ECONOMIC INSANITY

How Growth-Driven Capitalism Is
Devouring the American Dream

ROGER TERRY

Berrett-Koehler Publishers
San Francisco

Berrett-Koehler Publishers, Inc.
155 Montgomery St.
San Francisco, CA 94104-4109
Tel: 415-288-0260   Fax: 415-362-2512

Ordering Information
Individual Sales. Berrett-Koehler publications are available through most bookstores. They can also be ordered direct from Berrett-Koehler at the address above.

Quantity Sales. Special discounts are available on quantity purchases by corporations, associations, and others. For details, contact the "Special Sales Department" at the Berrett-Koehler address above.

Orders for college textbook/course adoption use. Please contact Berrett-Koehler Publishers at the address above.

Orders by U.S. trade bookstores and wholesalers. Please contact Publishers Group West, 4065 Hollis St., Box 8843, Emeryville, CA 94662; tel. 510-658-3453; 1-800-788-3123; fax 510-658-1834.

Printed in the United States of America

Printed on acid-free and recycled paper that is composed of 85 percent recovered fiber, including 15 percent postconsumer waste.

Library of Congress Cataloging-in-Publication Data
Terry, Roger, 1956–
    Economic insanity : how growth-driven capitalism is devouring the American dream / Roger Terry.
        p.   cm.
    Includes bibliographical references and index.
    ISBN 1-881052-32-X (alk. paper)
    1. Capitalism—United States.   2. United States—Economic conditions—1981– 3. United States—Social conditions—1980–
I. Title.
HC106.8.T473   1995
330.973'092—dc20   95–19047
                                                                     CIP

First Edition
      99   98   97   96   95   10   9   8   7   6   5   4   3   2   1

For my children and your children.

Contents

Acknowledgments

I owe special thanks to Berrett-Koehler founder and publisher Steven Piersanti, without whom this book would never have been written. He saw potential in a disjointed pile of half-baked, angry essays I sent him nearly four years ago and encouraged me to reach beyond myself in developing the ideas that eventually resulted in this book. Steve's hands-on editorial direction was as invaluable as it is rare in today's publishing world.

Thanks must also go to David K. "Kirk" Hart and Warner Woodworth, two colleagues and friends at the Marriott School of Management, who taught me through example that it is both acceptable and imperative to question the system from within.

Highest appreciation must be reserved, however, for those who have already explored many of the themes I address and have expanded my understanding during the past four years. Their names, appropriately, are listed in the references.

Last, but surely not least, I acknowledge and appreciate the love and support of my wife and children, who give the ideas behind the words a particularly urgent and personal meaning. Any good this book may accomplish is ultimately for them and for all others who will inhabit America's future and dream the American Dream.

Foreword

To describe this book's thesis as controversial is to dramatically understate the case. It raises fundamental questions about society that must be asked. In doing so, it will be unwelcome in many quarters where there has been an unspoken (and perhaps unconscious) conspiracy *not* to raise these questions.

In part, those questions have to do with society's ability to satisfy human desires. What individuals really want in their lives is not riches, titillating experiences, and material goods without limit. People have only seemed to want these goodies because they perceived them to be means to greater ends. Those ends, in fact, are intangibles, including a fulfilling and meaningful life, in adequate comfort, surrounded by loving family, good friends, and a supportive community, in a salubrious social and natural environment—all within a democratic society in which there is liberty, fairness, and justice under the rule of law, where everyone has "enough" food, shelter, health care, education, employment, personal security, and a good chance to create a desirable life.

To many people in this and other countries, these ends

appear to constitute an unreachable dream—a dream that seems even less achievable than it appeared to previous generations. A secure job and a home of one's own are harder to come by than they were for our parents. The physical environment seems on the whole to deteriorate despite well-meant attempts to keep it wholesome. Increased weapons possession and violent crime are on everybody's mind. Wealth seems increasingly to be concentrated in a few hands, while the vast majority experience decreasing economic security. Most people in the rich countries are at least dimly aware of the increased hostility felt by the world's poor as they perceive that the system appears to be rigged against them.

A deep disillusionment is rapidly setting in. The sought-after material instrumentalities not only fail automatically to assure the ends; it now appears, if we all insist on those particular means, that succeeding generations will have diminishing opportunities to achieve their similar goals.

The contradictions of modern society are increasingly apparent. We consider it good news when economic production and consumption have increased by another increment; yet because of the high correlation between economic activity and environmental degradation, the latter is invariably worsened by the former. We consider it good news when new markets open up in China or India; yet it is obvious that extending our Western consumption patterns to the rest of the world would have a staggering impact on the earth. The business press applauds when the merger of two giant aerospace companies yields multi-million dollar bonuses to top executives and eradicates tens of thousands of jobs. Extending free trade is supposed to benefit all, yet the emergence of a global economy, rather than eliminating poverty, has significantly widened the gap between rich and poor nations. Instead of affluence spilling over from the wealthy nations into the poorer ones, the exact opposite is occurring. Cities around the world are filled with those who came seeking opportunity and have instead joined the vast army of homeless, unemployed, illiterate, drug-ridden, derelict, and effectively disfranchised.

The environmental carnage, chronic poverty and hunger, inner-city wastelands, and widespread disillusionment are typically viewed as "problems," for which we (or the government) must find "solutions." The solutions proposed include new technologies, management practices, regulations, new agencies, and so on. But the solutions seem regularly to lag behind the problems, so that despite temporary local alleviations, on the whole the global crises are continually worsening. Furthermore, we are beginning to suspect that there is a fundamental illusion involved when what is proposed as a solution is more of what caused the problems in the first place (that is, more technology, bureaucracy, economic growth, and consumption).

We see a very different picture if we think of these crises not as problems, but as *symptoms* of an underlying malady. Only then are we able to look for the more fundamental dysfunction, and consider change at the level where it will really meet the challenge of our time. This shift in perception is what Roger Terry is aiming at, and the process of refocusing our vision is guaranteed to be not completely comfortable.

Our situation is a bit like that of the person who comes to the physician with a collection of ailments, asking to be made well. He admits that he finds his work very stressful, he likes his cocktails in the evening, he enjoys his three packs of cigarettes a day, and he tends to be a gourmand—and he doesn't want any of those things changed. We can easily see the absurdity of a patient who implores his physician to heal him, but insists that the doctor not interfere with his drinking, smoking, eating, or working habits. We are equally illogical, though, when we admit the seriousness of the nonsustainability of the modern world's present course, and yet insist that the cure be sought without disturbing our dedication to economic growth and productivity increase, our concepts of "reasonable" financial return on investment, our cavalier attitude toward nature as provider of "resources" and ultimate dumping ground for our wastes, and our measuring other people in terms of their economic usefulness.

Terry's argument can be summarized as follows. Imagine a short list of assumptions similar to those immediately above. Let us call this List A. Now imagine a list of the intangible goals that most people want in their lives, and the characteristics they desire of their society; call that List B. The disturbing thesis advanced by Roger Terry is that the assumptions of List A are fundamentally incompatible with, and can never lead to, the goals of List B.

Worse yet, his analysis is quite robust in the sense that it tends to hold despite minor differences in the two lists when they are created by different groups of people, even from different cultures. In other words, what Terry is revealing is a basic contradiction in modern society. Assumptions we all tend to buy into, and which appeared to work well for us in the past—assumptions with which our educating system (not only schools and universities, but also the media, the advertising industry, the Internet, and so forth) effectively indoctrinates each succeeding generation—are now in fundamental conflict with our concepts of a good society.

Increasingly, people in the modern world feel powerless and alienated, and no wonder. They ascribe these feelings to the failings of interest-group politics, or fanatical left-wing activists, or greedy capitalists, as is their inclination. Yet the real causes lie far deeper, and the culpability is far more widespread (since we all buy into the assumptions more than we may like to think). The liberal ideal is that all citizens should be guaranteed equal opportunity to reach their individual potential within the framework of a free and supportive society. But the economy has been allowed to control both collective and individual lives, to the detriment and diminishment of the dream. To reinstate the dream, economics must be put back into the political, moral, and social context where it belongs. And that requires a shift in very basic cultural assumptions.

The central question Terry raises is: How do we create the greatest good for all human beings while providing for their physical needs and wants? For Americans, this question is properly asked within the larger aim of the Founding Fathers— to create a society where the individual could freely seek a fulfilling *life*, an equal share of *liberty* within the bounds of democracy, and an independent sense of *happiness*. As he explains, the basic problem is that our society has come to be dominated by economic institutions, such that these goals tend to be thwarted.

Historically, as corporations became larger and more powerful, they also tended to become immune to social and moral strictures that held elsewhere. The organizational, moral, and social principles that we demand in all other facets of our association with each other are not expected to apply to economics. As a result, a large corporation can be self-interested, undemocratic, authoritarian, toxic to the true spirit of community, abusive, and amoral, and we accept this all as merely part of the price for having a free-market economy.

Business is largely an authoritarian arena, and it is so because of the way ownership is defined and distributed. Ownership turns out to be the key to why our economy and the

individual organizations that compose it are inherently authoritarian and often abusive to the people they employ; why
corporations are allowed to treat "human resources" as they
treat other resources—something to be used up and discarded;
why the economy seems beyond anyone's control.

Terry argues persuasively that fine-tuning the present capitalist system will not be enough to save our failing society.
The one thing that has power to bind us together again as a
people, says Terry, is a common purpose—the social, moral,
economic, and political ideal called the American Dream. This
involves giving all citizens the assurance of equality by return-
ing to them the power they have lost, or granting to them the
power they never possessed.

We will not correct the present system's inequities by
transforming the workplace or taking money from the wealthy
and giving it to the poor. Corporate reengineering, employee
empowerment, and all the other buzzwords we have dreamed
up quietly bypass the real issue, as do all liberal social redistribution programs. None of the currently popular approaches to
achieving greater equality and democracy in the workplace
addresses the fundamental obstacle to a free and equitable society: lack of true ownership.

Thus, the most fundamental shift required for alleviating
the many ills of the present system, says Terry, is a shift in our
unquestioned assumptions. And the most radical sociopolitical
shift concerns the patterns and prerogatives of capital ownership.

These issues are uncomfortable to contemplate. They are
uncomfortable primarily because we have refused to think
about them for so long. We want to have a sound and safe and
prosperous nation; and yet we also want to avoid challenging the
systems and programs and philosophies and amorality that are
leading us to the exact opposite conditions.

It is possible to identify a number of characteristics of a system that could actualize the American Dream: a no-growth economy, widespread capital ownership, self-limiting corporate growth, sensitivity to environmental quality, fewer work hours per week, technological development driven by real societal needs, less incentive for people to behave as predators and mercenaries, and more incentive for them to behave as cooperative members of a society with an overriding common goal of happy and peaceful prosperity.

The crucial question is "How do we get from here to there?" It will require short-term ameliorating measures plus long-term cultural and structural changes.

Roger Terry is not the first to propose that we need to have organizations that are communities of employee-owners, bound together by shared principles and noble goals. His analysis goes deeper than most, however, in showing how fundamental a political, social, and cultural change is involved, and in pointing out that the required emancipation from obsolete assumptions must take place one person at a time—starting with us. His arguments are thought-provoking. Even if he turns out to be only partly right, we need to pay attention to his challenge.

Willis Harman,
President of the Institute
of Noetic Sciences

Introduction

Powerless Over Our Future

If you believe the polls, ordinary Americans are concerned about the decay and disorder they see around them. No one, it appears, is able to do much to stop the deterioration, much less reverse it. In many ways, we the people feel powerless. Powerless over the economy. Powerless over our elected officials. Powerless over the ballooning national debt. Powerless over the moral malaise that is spreading like an epidemic. Powerless over a thousand social ills that are rising like a tidal wave to engulf us. Powerless, in short, over the future—*our* future.

When an entire people feels powerless over its future, this is an indication that democracy no longer exists in more than name, for in a democracy power resides in the people. Consequently, this sense of impotence and loss has spawned a wave of frustration that is growing in both size and intensity. The people know that something in America is broken, but they don't quite know what, they don't know why, and, most important, they don't know how to fix it. All they can point to are the symptoms.

The symptoms, of course, are evident everywhere. It is the illness itself we can't seem to put our finger on. And so all our solutions—from government wealth redistribution to corporate restructuring—are symptom-oriented, which means that they are by definition inadequate. Indeed, many of our so-called solutions create more problems than they cure. They attempt to alter the results of the system without changing the system that produces those results.

"Recent reports and analyses," writes Willis Harman, "have made it clear that *the global dilemmas are real and imminent*, and that these *will require fundamental system change* for their resolution—that further economic growth, technological application, modernization, shift to 'information society,' and so on are bringing additional problems more rapidly than solutions" (Harman, 1991, 2). The problem, in short, is not with how firmly the roof of our collective house is nailed on, or how well the walls are put together, or even how much we pay the carpenters. The problem is that we have been using the wrong blueprint.

Consequently, this book seeks to identify a new pattern, a new model, a new way of looking at our organizational and individual lives. And I believe that pattern can be found in an outright rejection of certain assumptions that drive our economic system, in reforming the parameters that govern our ability to own capital, and in embracing once-familiar ideals that we have abandoned in our hopeless quest to find happiness in a consumer society based on endless growth and accelerating scientific progress. The intent of this book, then, is to point out where we have gone astray, to remind us of the full and original *meaning* of the American Dream, and to engender the hope that that Dream is neither dead nor beyond our eventual reach.

Our economic system, we must acknowledge, is much more

than just a free market, a collection of businesses and bureaucracies, exchanges and transactions. At a more fundamental level, it is a common pattern of thought, a way of looking at the world around us, and it manifests itself in our financial dealings, our ownership practices, and our producer-consumer relationships. This pattern of thought pervades all we do. It envelops our lives in such a profound and subtle way that most of the time we're not even aware that it exists. It's just there, an inseparable part of us, as software becomes part of a computer, because we don't step back from it to consider it, or question it, or rewrite it.

Granted, stepping back from the economic system to get a clearer look at it isn't exactly easy. In some ways, it's like stepping back from the Milky Way galaxy to get a better view of its shape and dimensions. We can't do it literally, because we're stuck in the middle of it, but we must learn to step back figuratively, in our minds, and reassess its involvement—nay, its control—in our lives, because it is the economic *system* and not just the way we implement it that is flawed. If we are to solve the monumental problems that face us, we must change the way we think about things, because our problems are systemic in nature, and all our present attempts to solve them are as effective as straightening deck chairs on the *Titanic*.

Hitting a Wall

American businesses have gradually arrived at the conclusion that they must either change or die. The ultracompetitive global marketplace has no room in it for low-quality, outdated, slow-to-market, or high-cost products. Business leaders have figured out that in order to achieve high quality, competitive costs, speed to market, and world-class design, they must abandon the outmoded bureaucratic model of management and replace it with leaner, meaner organizational structures staffed with creative, intelligent, motivated workers.

I have spent a fair amount of time surveying the current management literature on change, and I invariably find the experience frustrating. Hundreds, perhaps thousands, of consultants and business leaders are pushing for what they see as dramatic reform. They want to reengineer the corporation, create excellent executives, empower the workforce, unleash the powers of democracy in organizational America, give workers a sense of ownership, develop intelligent organizations, and make every employee a leader. These are all worthy objectives and are definitely steps in the right direction. What frustrates me is that they all reach a certain point in both their theory and their application and suddenly they hit a wall. They never reach the logical conclusion to their own arguments.

Why is this so? For the simple reason that they are looking for answers *within* a system that doesn't work. The *wall* they hit is the outer limit of the current *system*. They reach that and can go no further. It's as though our current system of thought were their entire universe. They have never asked themselves what lies beyond its borders. Why do we assume that the answer lies in fixing certain aspects of the present system? Why don't we ever entertain the thought that perhaps it is the system itself that is lacking?

In the next few chapters I will question several major assumptions of the current system, and even if you don't agree with my analysis, I hope that you will come to see that in reality there is no wall. Beyond the comfortable confines of our current economic system, there is a whole universe of potential answers to our problems. Before we start questioning assumptions, though, we first need to look at an idea that is central to the arguments of this book, for it offers a clue as to what an ideal system should look like. Without an ideal, a correct map, and a destination, we shall find ourselves on a path to nowhere.

The American Dream

Just what exactly *is* the American Dream? Is it merely the opportunity to acquire wealth, to be at least comfortable and secure, if not outright affluent? If so, then there is nothing uniquely American about it. You can achieve it just as well in Germany or Australia or Hong Kong. We talk about the American Dream a great deal—it's a term we hear often—but usually all it means to us is some kind of nebulous level of financial well-offness, measured and merited on an individual basis. It has become an economic term, nothing more.

Not surprisingly, Ronald Reagan proclaimed this narrow vision of America: "What I want to see above all is that this country remains a country where someone can always get rich." This, of itself, is not such a bad desire, but to want this "above all" makes one wonder about Reagan's perception of America, wonder how many Americans share his tunnel vision of the nation's purpose and meaning.

My contention in this book is that the American Dream is—or should be—much more than a wealth wish. I base this argument on the notion that the dreams and ideals that guided the Founders were much more comprehensive than the simple fantasy of getting rich. They were after "a more perfect union," a nation to stand as an archetype for all the world. If ever there was a nation that stood for something, that had a manifest meaning and purpose—a mission—that nation was and is the United States of America.

The very notion of nationhood in our day might seem almost obsolete, irrelevant. Multinational corporations now stretch beyond geographical and political boundaries and wield wealth and power greater than many small countries. But countries and corporations exist for very different reasons and serve different purposes, even though some people have suggested that multinational corporations *are* the nations of the future. If this is true, then we can expect the demise of democracy and the rapid resurrection of political, and not just economic, tyranny.

Nations serve a distinct purpose in the world, and, ideally, that purpose goes far beyond wealth or race or religion or language or cultural heritage. We must not confuse nationhood with nationalism, which promotes an *us versus them* attitude and leads to all sorts of lunacy. If the bold experiment that began in Philadelphia in 1787 retains any credibility in our troubled world, nations *should* exist in order to "establish justice, insure domestic tranquility, provide for the common defence, promote the general welfare, and secure the blessings of liberty." The Founders were not interested in their own lives only. Rather, they were striving to create a "new order of the ages," a pattern for all nations and peoples and times, with America as the Great Experiment.

In spite of our heritage, however, we still seem collectively confused at times about the experiment we are supposedly performing. "What experiment?" we ask. "Isn't that water under the bridge? Wasn't that all settled long ago? Aren't we through experimenting?" But if the experiment is over, why is our freedom incomplete? Why is our democracy impotent? Why are we becoming more unequal and disunited? Why is the American Dream, even the narrowly defined economic dream, so difficult to achieve for so many? Maybe we don't understand the Dream as well as we should. Maybe we don't understand America very well.

If we go back to the source of the American Dream, the

ideals and values upon which this nation was founded, we find a number of key ideas—among them equality, liberty, democracy, unity, opportunity, morality, justice, prosperity, happiness, and individual dignity—abstract ideas for which our forebears were willing to sacrifice their very lives. Thomas Jefferson put it well: "We hold these truths to be self-evident, that all men are created equal, that they are endowed by their Creator with certain unalienable Rights, that among these are Life, Liberty, and the pursuit of Happiness." In broad strokes, Jefferson painted a picture of the American ideal, touched a nerve that moved his fellow Americans to action, that separated them, figuratively and literally, from every other people on earth and set them up as a pattern for other nations. His message rang loudly in their ears, just as it should ring in ours today: *All citizens of this great land are theoretically guaranteed an equal opportunity to reach their individual potential within the framework of a free and supportive society.*

It is this ideal that in theory gives U.S. citizens the liberty to become the most fully human people on earth. And it is this ideal that, in spite of our admitted imperfections, still draws people from all countries to the shores of America the Beautiful. For the most part, these immigrants don't come to get rich. They come to be free, to worship as they choose, to escape oppression in all its hideous forms, to take a hand in their own government, to be equal before the law, to walk with dignity, to make as much of their individual lives as they can. They come, in short, to be Americans. Not African-Americans, not Asian-Americans, not Irish-Americans, not Hispanic-Americans, not gay or straight Americans, not blue- or white-collar Americans, not conservative or liberal Americans, not upper- or middle-class Americans, and certainly not lower-class Americans. Simply Americans. For America is not merely a geographical region of the earth's crust; it is not only a unique political structure; it is not just a culture formed from the various ingredients that went into the melting pot. It is much, much more. America, above all, is an idea, an ideal that represents the very best in human nature and vision.

My belief is that our nation has gotten off track because we have divorced our economic concerns from the social and political ideals that guided the Founders. Consequently, our economy has grown up on the shaky foundation of several inherently false assumptions—unlimited ownership, boundless growth, ever-increasing productivity, accelerating technological advancement, and self-interested competition—and this foundation has created an unwieldy economic system that is drastically incongruous with every other aspect of our lives as Americans.

If you look at our American ideals—democracy, liberty, equality, unity, happiness, community, and so on—you find that both the structure and exercise of our economic system are in direct conflict with those ideals. Our businesses, by and large, are not democratic, nor do they create liberty; they do not foster either equality or unity; they supplant community; they limit true opportunity; and they treat individuals as commodities, mere *human resources* to be bought, used up, and replaced.

These are fundamental flaws in the structuring of our economic affairs, and no symptom-oriented, Band-Aid approach to treating them will make them go away. If we want an economic system that is congruent with our higher ideals, we must attack the root of the problem and stop hacking at the leaves. We must question the basic assumptions that drive the system and reveal them for what they are.

Modern America—with an economic system that directly conflicts with its social and political ideals—is like a car with its accelerator jammed wide open and its brakes locked at the same time. Not only is such a vehicle a nightmare to drive (just ask the president and Congress), but incredible internal damage can also result from the competing demands placed on the machine. This internal damage is evident, of course, in the vessels of government and commerce, but primarily in the lives of frustrated individual Americans who find it increasingly difficult to feel good about either their present situations or their future prospects.

Part 1

Questioning the System

When he was young Phædrus used to think about cows and pigs and chickens and how they never knew that the nice farmer who provided food and shelter was doing so only so that he could sell them to be killed and eaten. They would "oink," or "cluck," and he would come with food, so they probably thought he was some sort of servant.

He also used to wonder if there was a higher farmer that did the same things to people, a different kind of organism that they saw every day and thought of as beneficial, providing food and shelter and protection from enemies, but an organism that secretly was raising these people for its own sustenance, feeding upon them and using their accumulated energy for its own independent purposes. Later he saw there was: this Giant. . . .

The Giant began to materialize out of Phædrus' Dynamic dreams when he was in college. A professor of chemistry had mentioned at his fraternity that a large chemical firm was offering excellent jobs for graduates of the school and almost every member of the fraternity thought it was wonderful news. . . .

So here was this Giant, this nameless, faceless system reaching for him, ready to devour him and digest him. It would use his energy to grow stronger and stronger throughout his life while he grew older and weaker until, when he was no longer of much use, it would excrete him and find another younger person full of energy to take his place and do the same thing all over again.

—Robert M. Pirsig,
Lila: An Inquiry into Morals

Most of you [graduates] are here
[at commencement] today only because you
believe this charade will help you get ahead
in the world. But in the last few years things
have got out of hand; "the economy," once
the most important thing in our materialistic
lives, has become the only thing. We have
been swept up in a total dedication to "the
economy," which like . . . [a] massive
mudslide . . . is rapidly engulfing and
suffocating everything.

—Hugh W. Nibley,
"Leaders and Managers"

1

Feeding the Bastard Child

The original American Dream, the Dream that inspired the Founders, has diminished in our day. Indeed, it has shriveled from a grand and comprehensive social ideal to an economic wish list, a self-centered program of selective prosperity in which we make our mark as consumers, not as producers and creators. The economy has become our greatest concern—for the simple reason that we have allowed it to control both our collective and individual lives. Yet in the context of what America once meant, the economy is but one small part of a much larger ideal, an ideal that, sadly, we have shoved into the background.

This is not to say that economic matters are unimportant. Indeed, if the economy is ailing, all other aspects of the American Dream can't help but be affected. But a healthy economy alone will not restore the American Dream any more than giving an AIDS patient a million dollars will make him well again. Several other factors must first be put back into the American equation, for the Dream is not just economic—it is also *political* and *social* in nature. Instead of spending time and energy trying to make the economy more efficient, we ought first to put economics back into the social and political context where it rightly belongs.

In the day of Jefferson, Adams, and Washington, the economy was not the primary adhesive that held the people together. Indeed, economic differences almost prevented the thirteen original states from uniting into one country. Today, by contrast, it seems the economy is all that holds us together. In every other area of life, we find only divisiveness. The common ideals, values, and dreams that once united us as a people are fracturing and fading before our eyes. The only thing we agree on anymore is that America is in deep trouble, and the only thing that binds the Union together is our voracious economy.

Everything Is Economic Nowadays

Perhaps the best way to cut through the layers of complex theory, conflicting opinion, and thoughtless tolerance that obscure our view of this insatiable beast is to ask an almost insultingly simple question: *How do we best satisfy the physical needs and wants of human beings?* This is the fundamental question of economics, but unfortunately it is not as simple to answer as it is to ask. Indeed, seventy-odd years of East-West tension resulted from this question, for communism offered one answer (a strictly controlled, centrally planned economy) and capitalism another (a largely unregulated, profit-motivated market), and the world wasn't quite big enough for both perspectives. Even if we limit ourselves to market-based economic systems, the question is not easy to answer, for the market mechanism is both complex and controversial, fraught with disconcerting moral and social issues.

In spite of, or perhaps because of, its simplicity, this question, to my knowledge, is never expressed so directly in the economics courses offered at our colleges and universities. The reason it is not asked is because it is actually a moral and philosophical, not a mathematical, question, and economics has evolved into a mathematical science.

As a field of scholarly study, economics has distanced itself from real-world concerns and conditions to the point where it has become little more than an exercise in mental gymnastics, a discipline filled to overflowing with complex mathematical models constructed of Greek symbols and impossible, other-worldly assumptions. Economics, the science, is evident in the media-happy, everyday world where we live and work. Facts and figures constantly bombard us: unemployment, cost of living, consumer price index, business cycles, recessions, real wages, inflation, exchange rates, wealth distribution, poverty levels, GNP, GDP, leading indicators, lagging indicators, and so on, ad nauseam.

Economics has reached such a sterile plateau, in fact, that Robert Heilbroner asks in his classic *The Worldly Philosophers: The Lives, Times, and Ideas of the Great Economic Thinkers* whether there even *are* worldly philosophers anymore. And his answer is no. "There are certainly a vast number of economists," he says, "over twenty thousand of them in the United States alone. . . . There is a Nobel Prize for Economics. There are economists in every bank and corporation; there are economists in the newspaper columns in the morning and on the television broadcasts at night." But are there worldly philosophers? "Not if we mean by the term great prognosticators or great visionaries. . . . In the main, economics has become a technical, often arcane calling, and ambitious projections of imagination into the future are no longer listed among its aims" (Heilbroner, 1986, 322-23). Although there are notable exceptions, most economists today, even some Nobel Prize winners, are technicians, not philosophers.

Why is this so? Because the realm of economics has become a world unto itself, a world of numbers and equations that are becoming less and less relevant because they are no longer attached to the basic questions and issues that spawned the whole field of economics in the first place. Economic thought is now merely an analytical tool, not a guiding philosophy.

Even on the most practical level, economics has distanced itself from the real questions of life and is setting up its own ground rules. We speak of the "business world" because it *is* a world of its own, and it is consuming the larger world of which it used to be only a part. Sports, entertainment, the arts, politics, the media, medicine, law, education, charity, the family, human relationships—all are being devoured, partially digested, and regurgitated with an acrid economic flavor. Everything is economic nowadays, at least on the surface, and yet few seem willing to look beneath this veneer and ask the questions that troubled the great thinkers of past centuries, questions that make us evaluate our most basic assumptions. Especially since the demise of the Cold War, we have apparently assumed that all the fundamental questions of economics have been put to rest. Capitalism won, communism lost, end of story.

This, specifically, is where we have failed, for those questions have never been answered satisfactorily. The great worldly philosophers debated them and never arrived at a suitable answer. But now there are no great worldly philosophers, no inquisitive minds to attack the larger picture and make us rethink the inadequacies of our system at its most fundamental level. We are in the hands of technicians, who have no interest in a panoramic view.

This particular brand of myopia persists because we have anesthetized economics and severed it from its philosophical underpinnings, because we have interpreted the fundamental question of economics in terms of processes and techniques. *How do we best provide for the physical needs and wants of human beings?* The key word here is "best," which on those rare occasions when we bother with the larger view, we have interpreted to mean "most efficiently." But *best* can have a much broader meaning. We can define it in moral or philosophical terms. *How do we create the greatest good for all human beings while providing for their physical needs and wants?* That is a completely different question, one we have yet to answer. Neither communism nor capitalism in any of its various guises has addressed this question in a meaningful way.

Consequently, our present system contains no satisfactory answer. And yet that is exactly where we have been searching. For decades we have been tinkering with the knobs on an old black-and-white TV, moving the rabbit ears around, trying somehow to get a tolerable picture. It has apparently never occurred to us that what we need is a new color TV, or a cable hook-up, or maybe, heaven forbid, to throw the tube away for good and spend our spare time living life in the flesh and not vicariously. We need somehow to become uncomfortable with our present habits of thought and behavior.

The Bastard Child

As suggested by this chapter's epigraph, "the economy" has become our all-consuming interest. By elevating it above and divorcing it from our political and social aspirations, we have allowed the economy to get out of control—and by that I mean *out of our control*—to the point where it is now in control. The result is that, to a surprising degree, most Americans live under the yoke of a system from which they are more or less excluded. To be more specific, most Americans are noncapitalists living in a capitalistic system. You can be a noncapitalist in two ways: First, you can disagree philosophically with the basic premises of capitalism. This category is surprisingly small. Second, whether or not you believe the theory, in a practical sense you are not a capitalist unless you possess capital. This group is inordinately large.

Many Americans own stock in some corner of corporate America. But that does not necessarily make them capitalists. If we define capital as "accumulated goods devoted to the production of other goods," most stockholders cannot consider themselves capitalists just because they own a little stock. Their primary intent is not to produce goods with their capital. To them, investing their savings in corporate America is no different from putting their money in a six-month CD at the local bank. It's simply the prudent thing to do if you don't want inflation to get the best of you; and if the stock market isn't performing so well, then you sell your shares of stock and invest your hard-earned money in T-bills or municipal bonds or soybean futures—whatever pays the highest return. Frankly, these *passive* stockholders don't even care whether or not a product is produced. What they care about is the capitalist holy trinity of stock price, earnings per share, and dividends.

Most of these token capitalists are employees of corporations or small businesses. And, as such, they are not independent, they are bound—to their current employers and, more important, to the system. They can escape with relative ease and at any time from their respective employers—and either find a new employer or fight the exhausting self-employment battle—but they can't really escape the yoke the system puts on them, because they don't own capital.

These people are, in practice, noncapitalists, because they are *dependent*. Dependent on what? First and foremost, on their paychecks. But in the larger sense they are dependent on the ebb and flow of "the economy." Gone are the days when communities were more or less self-sufficient, when people didn't lose their jobs because of events or changing business practices in some other corner of the nation, or of the globe.

By contrast, let's assume for a moment that I am employed at a General Motors plant in middle America. If the economy takes a downturn, consumers across the nation will reduce or delay their car buying. Because of lower demand by people I shall never know but on whom I depend, I may lose my job when the plant closes, along with hundreds or thousands of my co-workers. But this is not the end of it. This is merely the stone that causes ripples to surge outward in the economic pond. The collective payroll of my closed plant will now be missing from the local economy. Retailers, small businesses, restaurants, and other services that depend on the disposable income of GM employees will be hurt. Many will fail. Tax revenues will shrink, causing hardship among teachers and other civil servants. Fewer people will have health insurance to cover their medical bills. Charity cases will increase at the hospitals, which will not only drain federal funds but also increase premiums for those who do still have medical insurance. And the ripples spread out further and further. We are all interconnected by "the economy."

Although their incentives naturally run toward perpetuating the system, even big-time capitalists aren't immune to the whims and fluctuations of "the economy," which is infinitely more potent even than the wealthiest billionaires. No one is immune, because our lives are shaped and misshaped by large, unwieldy, impersonal organizations. We've become one giant community—a community too large to maintain the balance that interdependence requires, too large to be governed effectively, too large to prevent the individual from being swallowed up in the needs of the impersonal whole, too large, indeed, even to be called a community. We are an "economy." That's what binds us together now, not community. Economic ties have supplanted social ones.

And yet "the economy" is nothing more than the bastard child of modern-day capitalism and the illegitimate assumptions that drive it. And now the bastard child is both in control and out of control, simply because we won't admit to ourselves that somewhere along the road to organizational dominion we sired it by our greed, our ignorance, our self-interest, and our desire for instant gratification. We won't claim responsibility for it, and therefore it isn't required to play by the same rules that govern individuals and made possible the birth of our nation.

Nevertheless, we are mortally afraid of disciplining "the economy." We simply feed it, make certain it keeps growing, regardless of how fat and insolent and burdensome it becomes to us as individuals. "The economy" even dictates our morals, for what is good for the economy, we are told, is good for the American people. This inverted moral imperative then filters on down to the organizational level and infiltrates our lives through the economic activities we pursue during most of our waking hours.

Organizational Morality

Because of the way our particular system has grown up, all that we see as good and desirable in people's lives—everything from canned beans and high-top basketball shoes to laptop computers and Beethoven on CD—comes from the large organizations of capitalism; therefore these organizations must survive, at all costs. And not only must they survive, they must prosper. They must guard themselves against any future possibility of failing. They must increase their assets, their profits, and their market share, at the expense of any competitors, or the environment, or even their own employees.

Organizations must grow, for if they do not grow, they become vulnerable and may fail. And if businesses fail, dire consequences follow: employees become unemployed, become a burden on society; "the economy" is harmed; consumers have less disposable income to buy the products they want and need; and our standard of living, that elusive economic measure of relative wellness, declines. Therefore, organizations must, absolutely must, prosper. This is the cardinal rule of "the economy," the highest law of economic America. Large organizations must not perish.

And because of this cardinal law, any act that enhances organizational success can be rationalized, because it works for the greater good of humankind, regardless how repugnant it may be to moral individuals. Thus, because we have exalted economic exigencies above political, social, or moral considerations, organizational morality now supersedes individual morality. Often it even supersedes the law.

Citing *U.S. News and World Report* statistics, Paul Hawken claims that 115 of the *Fortune* 500 were convicted of serious crime during the 1980s. No one knows how much misconduct went undetected, but the more important question is this: What was their punishment? Sometimes nothing. Sometimes a handslap, a fine, which can be written off as a business expense. Are they ever closed down, even after a long history of flouting the law? No. Union Carbide lives on, although many victims in Bhopal have not received even a penny of compensation. Indeed, "following the accident, Union Carbide proceeded to liquidate a substantial portion of its assets and give them out to shareholders in special dividends, thus reducing the corporation's potential payout to the victims" (Hawken, 1993, 116).

According to Russell Mokhiber, author of *Corporate Crime and Violence*, corporations kill 28,000 people and seriously injure another 130,000 every year by selling dangerous or defective products. More than 100,000 employees die each year because of exposure to toxins and other dangers at work (Mokhiber, 1988, 15). Are these organizations ever given the death penalty? No. Because the organization is more important than either the people it employs or the society it should serve.

Executives understand this. Middle managers understand this. The lowest-level employees understand this. Above all, the government understands this. Why? Because if the large organization fails, masses of people—both managers and employees—suddenly become "occupationally abandoned" and are at the mercy of the economy. This is why employees put up with the moral imperative of organizational survival; this is why they submit themselves to arbitrary authority; this is why they become "good corporate citizens." This is why no one demands that organizations play by the same rules and adhere to the same moral principles deemed appropriate for individuals.

The Founding Values

Tackling this separate and self-serving organizational morality head-on, David K. Hart argues that all organizations in our nation should be governed by what he calls the Founding values, for these values are congruent with human nature and ensure that people are productive and happy. "The Founders believed that the Founding values should guide all human institutions: Government, economic, and social institutions were bound to observe the same moral rules. They understood Adam Smith's argument that people become what they spend most of their lives doing. And if their lives never transcend the manufacture of pin heads, then there they stay" (Hart, 1988a, 6).

Hart bases this argument of organizational responsibility on three notions: that organizations exist to better the human condition (not vice versa), that human happiness is the ultimate goal of society, and that this happiness can only be achieved where organizations honor a certain transcendent moral truth.

"It is quite risky to suggest a single moral *a priori* that guided the Founders," he admits, "but I believe it can be argued that everything was based upon an extended meaning of the first word in the Jeffersonian triad of 'life, liberty, and the pursuit of happiness.'" That extended meaning is, quite simply, *the absolute sanctity of each individual's life.* "As free agents, individuals can magnify or squander the possibilities of their lives, but those lives are sacred. Therefore, no organization, public or private, has any right to deny, or even trivialize, the possibilities of individual lives with organizational requirements" (ibid., 5). With this statement, Hart brings to light a pivotal question: *Which is more important, the organization or the individuals in it?* The form of government the Founders established suggests their answer to this question. Unfortunately, we have turned their wisdom on its head and have permitted a different answer to shape our lives in modern America.

The Individual

Implicit in the notions of liberty, democracy, equality, morality, justice, happiness, human dignity, and even material prosperity is the fundamental concept—the bedrock, if you will—upon which the American Dream was built: that the individual is more important than any particular organization, including the nation itself, to which he or she belongs. *Belongs.* The word implies ownership. Does the individual really belong to an organization, or does the organization belong to the individuals who devote pieces of their lives to it? That is a question we must address as Americans, for the answer tells us where power really resides in this country.

If the individual is, in practice as well as in theory, more important than the organizations in his or her life, then organizations exist to serve society, never to be served by it. Jefferson suggested this arrangement in the statement that follows his assertion of unalienable rights: "That to secure these rights, Governments are instituted among Men, deriving their just powers from the consent of the governed. That whenever any Form of Government becomes destructive of these ends, it is the Right of the People to alter or to abolish it, and to institute new Government." If the government (or any other organization) becomes burdensome rather than of service to the people, it is their right to change or even do away with it.

If individuals are truly more important than organizations, then the people have the power to abolish any institution that proves abusive or even ineffective and replace it with a better one. The fact that every corporation in this land is granted a charter by the government and cannot exist without that express permission also suggests that the people have every right to revoke that charter should the corporation either break the law or endanger the lives or health of individuals. Indeed, in the latter part of the eighteenth and most of the nineteenth centuries, states regularly revoked the charters of corporations for abusing the powers granted them by the people. "Even when corporations met charter requirements, legislatures sometimes decided not to renew those charters" (Grossman and Adams, 1993, 21).

The people were cautious about granting corporate charters, determined to maintain control over these impersonal business entities and to ensure that they served society, not the other way around. "The colonists did not make a revolution over a few bags of tea," Richard Grossman and Frank Adams observe. "They fought for many reasons but chiefly to create a nation where citizens were the government and ruled corporations" (ibid., 18).

Times have indeed changed. Why, to put it bluntly, do corporations that flout the law with impunity still exist? Why do we put up with organizations that spend millions of dollars lobbying Congress to ease restrictions on pollution; that cheat the military on defense contracts; that defraud the public with lavish spending and fast-and-loose investment schemes; that deceive government about product safety; that render sterile hundreds of foreign employees who must work with chemicals banned in America; that worry more about profits than about human life; that are repeatedly convicted of violating health, environmental, and safety standards? Is it perhaps because they have become not only more powerful but also more important than the individuals they harm?

If this is true—if organizations are in fact more important and more powerful than the individuals either in or around them—then *people* are at the mercy of *things*; individuals become mere functions in the inexorable arithmetic of organizational survival, and pretty much anything can be justified. This, I suggest, is exactly the state of affairs in America today, and this explains why an increasing number of Americans are so frustrated, why we often feel we are something less than fully human, why the American Dream is diminished.

When I assert that individuals are more important than the organizations in their lives, I am not arguing for reckless and irresponsible individualism. The individual is not intended to live in isolation, heedlessly pursuing selfish interests at the expense of everyone and everything else. Indeed, the American Dream, which is, among other things, a *social* ideal, can only be achieved in collective settings. In essence, you can't be equal alone; you can't have a democracy of one; you can't be unified with just yourself. You have to have others to whom you are equal, with whom you can unite, who serve and are served by you in a collective effort to maximize each individual's potential.

This is what America is all about. But somewhere along the path that lies between our nation's founding and our present-day mess, we went astray. Somewhere we adopted the idea that people exist to serve the systems and groups and organizations in which they find themselves. People have become tools, *human resources*, to use the awful modern metaphor. The collective, then, is of a higher order than, and even defines, the individual. Consequently, we do not possess the power to determine the shape and contour and terrain of our lives. We are pawns on someone else's chessboard. And increasingly, that chessboard is an economic board, for economic matters have come to dominate our lives as individual Americans, to both define and constrict our dreams.

This should never be. As John Steinbeck so aptly expressed it: "Man . . . grows beyond his work, walks up the stairs of his concepts, emerges ahead of his accomplishments" (Steinbeck, [1939] 1982, 164). Work has a practical purpose—to provide food, clothing, and shelter for the individual in society—but work is something more than mere utilitarian labor. Work has purposes beyond the economic fruits it produces. Work helps individuals define themselves, define their place in the world, fix their unique stamp upon the physical, social, intellectual, or cultural environment. And this is the danger of placing other American ideals lower in our estimation than our economic needs and wants: *When the acquisition of wealth or even basic necessities becomes our primary objective, the individual, by definition, is less important than the work he or she performs and thus becomes a mere resource to be used by the organizers of economic endeavor.* Somehow we have reversed our fundamental moral position about which is more important, the organization or the individual.

If the Founders lived in our economy-worshipping society, where moral relativism and situational ethics define our organizational morality, they would likely be seen as arrogant, egotistical, or (heaven forbid!) politically incorrect. "Yet," Hart insists, "with their passionate hatred of unaccountable power and their commitment to liberty, such moral relativism would have been anathema, because it leaves people unprotected from arbitrary power exerted in their lives by organizations. That was unacceptable to them" (Hart, 1988a, 6).

Arbitrary power, unaccountable power. These are unflattering expressions, yet they precisely describe the type of power exercised by many individuals and virtually all organizations in our present system. And until we understand why this is so and what it means for us as individuals, we shall achieve neither our full potential as human beings nor a full measure of freedom and democracy as a people. Why is it that we do not demand freedom and democracy in our economic as well as our political affairs? Do we need another revolution?

As suggested earlier, the economy is both out of control and in control. And the longer we simply feed it, permit it to grow as fat as it can, we as individuals will be at its mercy. Inequality will continue to increase, and liberty and democracy will continue to shrink. The only way we can regain control of our economic lives is by questioning some of the most basic assumptions that drive our present system.

*The small volume of saving by the
average man, and its absence among
the lower-income masses, reflect faithfully
the role of the individual in the industrial
system and the accepted view of his function.
The individual serves the industrial system
not by supplying it with savings and the
resulting capital; he serves it by consuming
its products. On no other matter, religious,
political, or moral, is he so elaborately
and skillfully and expensively instructed.*

—John Kenneth Galbraith,
The New Industrial State

2

Consumerism: A Perfect Circle
That's Empty in the Middle

B efore I address the topic of consumerism and the problems that arise from placing this enormous burden on a shrinking middle class, let me backtrack a little and make an observation. If we are to solve our deeper social and economic problems, we must reverse our thinking about growth and prosperity and start imagining ways in which we as a society can attain a comfortable degree of prosperity without having all our economic activities be dependent on endless growth. Perhaps the first step in this rethinking process is to come to grips with one simple fact about *progress*, the philosophical doctrine that undergirds our growth imperative: *Progress is a journey without a destination.*

Goalless Movement
In *The True and Only Heaven*, Christopher Lasch debunks the notion that our belief in progress stems from either the Christian

doctrine of the millennium, that thousand-year period of peace preceding the end of the world, or the ubiquitous secular ideal of utopia, a perfect society toward which all human beings should be striving. It is not my purpose here to recite Lasch's arguments against the supposed millennial or utopian roots of progress. Suffice it to say that the fundamental distinction between our present-day conception of progress and the older notions of utopia and the Christian millennium is that the last two are end conditions, goals to guide our footsteps in the present. They are destinations toward which we are (or should be) traveling. Not so with progress. Progress has no destination, no culmination in something perfect or even desirable.

Progress is never satisfied. It assumes that what we have is never enough. We must continue to accumulate and consume, accumulate and consume, forever and ever, with no upper limit. This, of course, is insanity of the highest order. But the idea of progress is open-ended. It always looks beyond the present to the next step. It denies the existence of such a thing as the *good life* and focuses only on bettering our current state. But if there is no goal, no ideal to direct us, how do we know what progress even is? How do we know we are improving, moving forward instead of backward? Well, we don't. Movement is all that matters. Direction is a nonissue. This is why so much of our material progress is accompanied by social and moral deterioration.

And this is the fatal flaw of the progressive ideology: it cannot admit to an ideal. It cannot say, "This is good," for then the chance would exist that we might actually achieve that *good*, and progress would necessarily come to an end. But the doctrine of progress assumes we shall never arrive anywhere.

Progress can never answer the question "Where are we going?" because any answer would concede the existence of a destination, an ideal, a perfect pattern we are trying to achieve.

It would also admit to certain moral absolutes, such as goodness, truth, and happiness. So, in the absence of moral certainty and a specifically desired destination, how can we possibly know we are "making progress"? We can't. Such knowledge is impossible.

The only evidence of progress is movement. Not movement toward something, just movement. Any movement is better than no movement at all. And the more technically quantifiable that movement is, the easier it is to document. This is why we measure our progress in terms of technological advancement and scientific breakthroughs and the size of the economy instead of by how compassionate or cooperative or moral or happy we are. Measurement is everything where progress is concerned, and such intangible attributes are nearly impossible to measure.

This is why good is a nonconcept in our progress-minded world. *Good* can't be measured. *Better*, on the other hand, can be measured, because it compares two different things. But in the absence of an ultimate destination, how do we know which of two different things is better? We don't. And so to get around this obstacle the ideology of progress quietly embraces one unusual absolute: more. *More is better*. This axiom lies at the core of our belief in progress, and yet, strangely, this one absolute is in perfect harmony with the relativistic idea of endless progress, for *more* is never a final destination. By definition, it implies instability, insatiability, expansion, and obsolescence.

Indeed, the governing reality in the progressive dogma is the notion of obsolescence. Every advance shall be superseded by a new advance. *Nothing is best, because everything can be exceeded and, therefore, nothing is certain*. "That nothing is certain," says Lasch, "except the imminent obsolescence of all our certainties—our scientific theories, our technology, our artistic styles and schools, our philosophies, our political ideals, our fashions—naturally gives rise to the sense of impermanence that has been celebrated or deplored as the very essence of the modern outlook" (Lasch, 1991, 48). Impermanence, you might say, is the one permanent fixture in our progressive lives.

The upshot of this reasoning is that in terms of the rationale of progress, there can be no such thing as an American Dream. The Dream vanishes in the wake of an endless and measurable parade of technological innovations, because progress allows no ideals, no desirable and attainable stations where we can stop our goalless march and simply declare, "This is good. This is what civilization is supposed to be like. Let's stay here forever."

Endless Upgrades

Let's look at an example of the insanity spawned by the progressive ideology. An interesting scenario has been playing itself out in the software industry. WordPerfect and Novell, two companies headquartered in the valley where I live, recently merged, creating the third largest firm in the industry. They saw this as the best, perhaps even the only, option for staying in a game increasingly dominated by Microsoft. Novell and WordPerfect are not alone. Adobe and Aldus are joining forces, as are Electronic Arts and Broderbund. Consolidation is typical in this industry, as it is in many others. If companies do not grow, they die, and the easiest (and certainly the quickest) way to ensure future growth is to merge, to become instantly as large as possible.

The only problem with this is that ultimately growth in the software industry rests on only two pedestals: (1) new applications and (2) upgrades of existing applications. Unfortunately, both pedestals have inherent limitations. How many new applications do consumers really need? And how many can they afford? Likewise, why should consumers buy an upgrade when the current, "obsolete" version has more bells and whistles than they'll ever use? Take me, for example. I am using WordPerfect 5.1 for DOS to write this book. Depending on how you count, it's either one or two full steps—and soon will be three or four—below the current top-of-the-line upgrade. Sure, I'd like to have WordPerfect 6.0 for Windows, but my current version has more features than I'll ever use. Besides, I can't afford an upgrade. What happens when most users reach my situation?

The growth imperative is illogical, yet Microsoft, WordPerfect, Novell, and all their competitors are caught in its irresistible pull. They must create demand out of thin air, especially for upgrades that people don't need. Why? Because if they don't, the competition will. Then they will lose market share. This example holds true for most other industries also, whether you're talking about electronics or automobiles.

Perhaps no one else sees it this way, but it seems to me that most companies in these endless-upgrade industries have some- how misplaced the reason for their existence. They don't see the company's *primary* purpose in (1) providing a good working environment for members of the community, (2) bringing pros- perity to the community by selling a quality product, or (3) serving society in general. Their primary purpose has evolved into an imperative to grow, even if growth means selling products no one needs. But the reasons for this growth rest snugly in the arms of self-interest. It is not good enough anymore for a company to produce a quality product, offer good working conditions for many members of the community, or serve society. It must become the biggest, the best. Market share is everything.

Can every company in a given industry afford to embrace this self-centered philosophy? No, because for every company that gains market share, there is another that must lose market share. But in this intricate dance of organizational survival called capitalism, every company is driven by the growth imperative.

This, however, is a false, illogical, immoral imperative. The economy simply cannot grow indefinitely. Every industry in the economy cannot grow indefinitely. Every company in an industry cannot grow indefinitely. Technological progress cannot play itself out in an endless panorama of repeated obsolescence and perpetual replacement. This is a bankrupt economic philosophy that will reach its logical conclusion in relatively short order. We cannot afford such insanity. No society can. And yet we are hell-bent on pursuing this course, regardless of what either reason or the hard facts tell us.

We consumers must continue to buy things we don't really need—endless upgrades of nonobsolete products and a perpetual parade of new "stuff"—and we must consume it in increasing quantities. If we do not consume, overcapitalized businesses can't make a profit, they lay off workers, disposable income contracts, consumption falls even lower, and a particularly insidious cycle kicks in. And yet, as unbridled capitalism unwinds along its inevitable course, we consumers are less and less able to consume enough to maintain high enough levels of economic growth.

As I write, the economy is riding the momentum of a four-year-old recovery, but the closer one looks at this recovery, says *Time* magazine, "the more it appears to be unlike any in recent memory. It is a split-level surge in which mass layoffs are continuing side by side with new hiring and heavy overtime; high-income people are making more money, while many others are working at worse jobs for lower wages than a few years ago and still others have seen pay raises, if any, fall behind even today's slow (2.5 percent) pace of inflation" (Church, 1994a, 30).

National polls show that as many as 40 percent of the workforce think the nation is still in a recession. There has been no recovery in their personal economies. Even President Clinton admits that "this appears to be a recovery for investors." That's a nice way of saying that the capitalists are getting richer, while everyone else is getting left further behind. More and more people can't make ends meet, and myriad others are using up savings and going into debt to maintain a subsistence level of consumption. Let's not fool ourselves into thinking that we're going to recover from this economic malaise. Its source lies deeper than our repeated recessions and recoveries, which, like waves on the sea, are merely indicators of more profound forces.

Perhaps Bertrand de Jouvenel was right when he suggested that "societies are governed in their onward march by laws of which we are ignorant" (Jouvenel, [1948] 1962, 378) Maybe the dynamism that "carried them to their prime" is the same force that leads them to their doom. Perhaps there is nothing we can do about our addiction to progress and the illusion that we can pursue it like an ever-retreating pot of gold at the end of the technological rainbow. Still, I would like to think we can change course before it's too late, that we the people can regain control of our wayward nation and rein in the extreme economic, political, and social philosophies that are driving us to the precipice.

Of the two opposing political orientations popular in America today, theoretically, you would expect the liberals to believe in progress, which they do. But Lasch points out the inherent paradox of a "movement calling itself conservative" that doesn't "associate itself with the demand for limits," and not only on economic growth, but also on "the conquest of space, the technological conquest of the environment, and the ungodly ambition to acquire godlike powers over nature." (Lasch, 1991, 39). Liberals and conservatives alike have always worshipped at the altar of unending technological progress. And progress, Lasch contends, has become our secular religion.

Contrary to the Christian millennial vision that it replaced, the gospel of progress has no culmination, no utopia or paradise in which mankind will find rest from the competitive arena, from the mercenary world of commerce. Progress simply goes on forever, changing, growing, consuming everything in its path. The reason the secular theology of progress does not aim toward some ultimately desirable and happy ending is because its roots are not religious. They lie rather in the soil of moral relativism, agnostic science, and economic Darwinism. Human society, as a species, is adapting and reshaping itself, but not with any particular end in mind. Survival is our only motive, and the process—progress—is all that matters. We are pursuing a means without an end. But that means will indeed have an end, an unexpectedly abrupt and tragic one—unless we mend our ways.

Consumerism

The notion that progress does not have any noble objective or purpose bothers most people, when they take time to think it through carefully. Even George Bush (or one of his speechwriters) expressed dismay at the idea in his 1989 inaugural address: "What is the end purpose of this economic growth?" he asked. "Is it just to be rich? What a shallow ambition. Is there really any satisfaction to be had in being the fattest country? . . . What will they say of us, the Americans of the latter part of the twentieth century? That we were fat and happy? I hope not."

But what is the purpose of endless economic growth? What is the purpose of all our progress? According to our modern, technological definition, it has none. Progress is not actually taking us anywhere; it is merely a joyride we have pursued for the sake of what we might see and experience along the way. If, in the end, it deposits us back at the very beginning, where our journey began, then that, we must concede, is as good a place as anywhere else.

And what exactly do we experience along the way? The only experiences that count in the current progressive ideology are those we buy. Consumption is the name of the game, because consumption keeps the whole mechanism moving. Not only must we consume at ever-increasing levels to perpetuate the ride (like buying ticket after ticket at the amusement park so that we can go in circles until we're dizzy and nauseated), we must also consume because without consumption our lives would be empty. With no end destination to all this growth and progress, we can achieve satisfaction only through the "ride," through the illusion that we are going somewhere and experiencing something worthwhile. Laurence Shames decries modern consumerism as consumption without justification, without purpose:

> During the past decade, many people came to believe there didn't have to be a purpose [for consumption]. The mechanism didn't require it. Consumption kept the workers working, which kept the paychecks coming, which kept the people spending, which kept inventors inventing and investors investing, which meant there was more to consume. The system, properly understood, was independent of values and needed no philosophy to prop it up. It was a perfect circle, complete in itself—and empty in the middle. (Shames, [1989] 1991, 80-81)

Consumer-based, progress-driven capitalism is completely amoral. It must be. If our economic system were governed by a well-defined morality—say, for instance, that corporations were required to abide by the man-made laws that hold individuals in check or the absolute laws that regulate nature—it would die. It is, in fact, capitalism's amorality that makes it so strong. It professes no inherent need to bend either its methods or its motives to conform to any but the most forceful external moral restraints. The sole purpose of capitalism is to provide goods for consumption, at ever-increasing levels.

John Maynard Keynes proclaimed that such abundance would produce a "decent level of consumption for everyone" and would free people to pursue more important noneconomic interests (see Lasch, 1991, 74, 536). The flaw in his reasoning is that capitalism can't settle for a "decent level of consumption." Its dependence on progress and growth dictates that consumption must increase without end. Hence, a "decent" level of consumption is always "a bit more than what I now consume."

What this means is that production, likewise, will always increase. We can never say, "We've arrived. This is enough productive capacity." *More is always better.* The engine of capitalism is specifically designed to create profits and turn those profits into new capital—forever. The engine may burn out, or we may turn it off, but it will never create something other than what it was designed to create. And what capitalism is designed to create is an increasingly capitalized world, a world filled to overflowing with both products and production capacity. More factories, more equipment, more products, for ever and ever. And we must consume everything that is produced. That is the other side of the coin.

A Nation of Consumers

Because we are expected to consume everything that capitalism produces, America has evolved from a nation of citizens (who are so necessary in maintaining a republic) into a nation of consumers (who are essential only in maintaining an economy). Consumerism is our second job, you might say. "One of the most pervasive myths in contemporary society," write William G. Scott and David K. Hart, "is that, regardless of what people must do on the job, when they leave work, their time is their own. . . . The sacrifices and responsibilities that organizational obedience entails are amply rewarded by salaries that enable people to exploit their leisure time to the fullest. This is a cruel deception."

They go on to explain that, even though the range of options is great, what one does away from the job is also determined to a large degree by the needs of profit-seeking organizations. This predetermination of leisure activities is a logical extension of the organizational imperative: "that all behavior must enhance the health of modern organizations. . . . The rule is: *The primary obligation of the individual off the job is to consume*" (Scott and Hart, 1989, 72).

One largely unrecognized difficulty with this obligation, however, is that even though "we call ourselves consumers, . . . we do not [really] consume. Each person in America produces twice his weight per day in household, hazardous, and industrial waste, and an additional half-ton per week when gaseous wastes such as carbon dioxide are included" (Hawken, 1993, 12). Perhaps what we need is not just a redefinition of our purpose as citizens of this nation, but a redefinition of basic terms, such as *production* and *consumption*.

If we were to redefine production to mean the creation of either fully consumable or easily reusable products, rather than simply the churning out of quantifiable, purchasable stuff, and redefine consumption to mean the judicious acquiring of life-sustaining, rather than lifestyle-enhancing, goods and services, we might begin to rein in the rampant growth imperative that governs corporate America and threatens to destroy our society.

We toss about the term *economy*, as if all it meant were an expanding smorgasbord of delectables to consume, but *economy*, in the more original sense, refers to the thrifty, efficient, frugal use of resources. Our "economy," ironically, has come to represent the exact opposite of this original definition. It is, in fact, so *uneconomical* that its profligacy is consuming us.

*Growth of healthy organisms is
a natural phenomenon, but unregulated
and unlimited growth is found in nature only
in cancers that ultimately destroy their hosts
and themselves. We are creating an unregulated
economic system that has become the equivalent
of a cancerous tumor, and its unfortunate host
is human society. In the name of free markets,
prosperity, and democracy, modern society
is embarked on a path that ultimately can
lead only to the destruction of all three.*

—David C. Korten,
"A Deeper Look at
'Sustainable Development'"

3

Not Everything
That Grows Is Good

In their book, *The Second American Revolution*, James Patterson and Peter Kim give a somewhat outdated analysis of our recent economic woes, then present four widely divergent plans for strengthening the economy—one promoted by Lester Thurow, another backed by Robert Reich, a plan devised by the Council on Competitiveness, and, finally, Jack Kemp's proposed return to supply-side economics. Though individual pieces of each plan have some merit, all four are based on the assumption that economic health is a function of growth. If American companies can just become more competitive, the economy will grow, and everything will be all right.

Well, American companies in general have become, or are rapidly becoming, very competitive, the economy is growing once again, but everything is not all right. The problem is that we are looking for answers in the wrong place. We are trying to find solutions within a system that makes sense in the short term but is illogical for the long haul. We need systemic change, not just a more efficient economic machine.

Why should we want a different system, though? Isn't the current arrangement good enough? Perhaps we can find the answers to these two questions by asking two related questions: *Is it possible for the modern capitalist economy to grow forever, without hitting any kind of ceiling?* and *Is limitless growth a good thing?* My contention is that our continued belief in the assumption of limitless growth will bring catastrophic results. At some point, growth comes only at a tremendous price to society. Further, the capitalist economy simply cannot grow forever. It has built-in limits, and both economic and environmental ruin is the price of ignoring them.

Cancerous Growth

Every economic plan I've ever seen begins with the assumption that growth is necessary for a healthy society. Herman E. Daly and John B. Cobb, Jr., point out that although economists, like other scientists, claim to be value-neutral, "their shared values are [in fact] easy to identify. They are, above all, for economic growth. To challenge that as a goal is to place oneself outside the community [of economists]" (Daly and Cobb, [1989] 1994, 131). But what if growth is no longer the panacea it once was? What if our economy has grown to the point where its size and continued growth are actually hazardous to our social and economic health? What if the answer is not growth? If so, then the community of economists has been asking the wrong questions, which means that all their answers are also wrong. It is not the way the system functions or malfunctions that is the problem; it is the assumptions upon which the system rests and that have guided its evolution.

As David Korten points out in the epigraph to this chapter, not everything that grows is good. Indeed, the only instances of unlimited growth found in nature are cancerous tumors, which grow by stealing sustenance from healthy tissue, by fooling the immune system, by deceiving nearby cells into forming food-bearing vessels and producing growth-enhancing chemicals, and by opening new pathways for the malignancy to spread throughout the body. In essence, cancer tricks the body so that it actually contributes to its own destruction.

The unlimited-growth assumption makes capitalism similar in many respects to cancer. It creates economic growth at the expense of health in other areas of social concern. And as it becomes entrenched, it converts the surrounding society into a support structure for its continued growth. Everything becomes economic, and self-perpetuation becomes the guiding rule of the economic system.

Is there an alternative, though? Can we even imagine an economic system not dependent on perpetual growth? I suggest that we must begin to think along those lines, because the growth assumption is fast reaching the end of its long, long rope.

Let me introduce three arguments against limitless economic growth that may help put this issue in perspective. The first argument is simple and straightforward and has been presented in greater detail by others who have a more specific interest in environmental matters. The last two are more theoretical in nature, but point to an inherent flaw, an internal illogic in our system of unlimited capital ownership that suggests we must look beyond the present system.

The Environmental Argument

Kenneth Lux points out that our capitalist economic theory does not concern itself with human needs. In economics, *need* is a nonword. Economists are interested only in *wants*, or demand. "An important thing about *wants*," says Lux, "is that they are ultimately infinite and therefore unsatisfiable." Add to this the overall objective of conventional economics, which is to satisfy these wants, and a paradox emerges.

> It appears that economics has construed itself so as to attempt to accomplish the impossible: to satisfy that which cannot be satisfied. . . . From this we can start to see that economics, even at the level of its theory, may have something to do with why we are destroying our natural world.
> We live on a finite planet. If human beings are defined as being made up of infinite wants, and the task of an economic system is to fulfill that infinity, then such a system will go on endlessly churning out goods in an attempt to reach what is from the beginning an impossible goal. When the infinite production of goods meets up with a finite planet there is bound to be a collision. (Lux, 1990, 9)

If we were to imagine the traditional capitalist system as a container for wealth and consumable products, its shape would be that of an inverted cone, extending forever upward and outward. The growth assumption insists that we can keep pouring time, energy, and natural resources into the cone in the form of consumable products, and that it will never be full, never overflow. It will simply hold everything, forever. This, however, is an utterly irrational assumption.

Environmental factors alone should convince us that eventually two things will happen: (1) we shall run out of various natural resources to pour into the economy, and (2) we shall discover that all along the cone has not been self-contained, that it has been leaking toxins, contaminating the world around it, creating an enormous, costly mess.

Both economists and businesses have always operated on the assumption that the future will be similar to the past, that since the capitalist economy has grown over time, it will continue to grow. They don't consider the possibility that as the economy grows, it encounters constraints that were irrelevant when it was small. We might liken the economy to a seven-foot-six basketball player who had no trouble with doorways or finding clothes that fit when he was ten. But at twenty he has to duck to leave a room or to dodge light fixtures and must special-order pants, shirts, and shoes. The minimal impact of industrialization on the environment when the earth was a seemingly infinite, sparsely populated place has little relevance to our present circumstances. Times change. We cannot logically expect the effects of the ever-expanding capitalist economy to remain negligible.

"If capitalism has one pervasive untruth," declares Paul Hawken, "it is the delusion that business is an open, linear system: that through resource extraction and technology, growth is always possible, given sufficient capital and will. In other words, there are no inherent limits to further expansion, and those who wish to impose them have a political agenda. . . . [But] ever-expanding abundance is not a theory based on science, or history, or nature. It is based solely on self-interest" (Hawken, 1993, 32-33).

Capitalism's Imperialist Tendencies

John Hobson, a frail little Englishman with a speech impediment and a penchant for economic heresy, argued a century ago that in order to grow, indeed, in order to survive, capitalism had to become imperialistic. Without exporting both production capacity and products abroad, he maintained, capitalism will eventually suffocate itself. At the time, no one really took him seriously except the Marxists, who twisted his ideas into a strange confirmation of their own misconceptions. But Hobson's reasoning was both fascinating and deceptively simple: growth, the very engine that drove capitalism, also created a situation in which a nation could never consume everything it produced.

The poor, Hobson argued, didn't have the means to buy their fair share, and the rich had too much money to consume their proportion of the nation's production. Someone with a million-dollar income couldn't (or wouldn't see any reason to) buy a thousand times more consumer goods than a person with a thousand-dollar income. In fact, the wealthy in every society are mindful of what they *don't* spend, for if they spend all they have, they are no longer wealthy. Wealthy people, because they both want to and have to, save a good portion of their excess, but those savings must be put to use. If they are invested in new production capacity, which they usually are, it only compounds the problem, says Hobson. If society is already having difficulty consuming all it produces, then this perpetual increase in production capacity will only flood an already saturated market.

In order to grow, Hobson concludes, capitalist economies must not only invest their capital abroad, they must also sell their increased production abroad. They must export more than they import. From one nation's perspective, this provides a temporary solution for the necessarily imperialist capitalist economy, but in the long run it ruins a world economy, as more and more nations need an outlet for their excesses.

Hobson's ideas, although largely forgotten, are nonetheless significant, especially when seen in the light of American expansion after World War II. Because it was the dominant and, for a long time, the only real economic power on the block, America was able to fill the world not only with factories and production equipment, but also with Coca-Cola and Levi's and Chevrolets. We ran large trade surpluses. And at home our standard of living shot skyward. There was no underconsumption to bog down our economic growth, because we sent excess production abroad and real wealth was our most significant import.

Predictably, though, the rest of the world began to catch up with us, even surpass us. We tend to see this as a tragedy, of course, for many of our industries have either failed or lost their competitive edge, but it had to happen. We could not expect to live forever in the unreal economic conditions that prevailed after World War II. Now the tables are turned. Japan and Korea and Germany and other countries are investing in America, selling us their excess production, pursuing the same policy of economic imperialism that gave us such prosperity in the 1950s and 1960s. And we have a huge trade deficit, for we insist on overconsuming in an environment that suggests we should actually be underconsuming. Somehow, we're actually consuming much more than we produce. How is this possible?

It's simple, really. We have found a way around Hobson's insistence that capitalist societies cannot consume all they produce without becoming imperialistic: debt. We are buying on credit. Not only is the trade deficit healthy and growing, but consumer debt accounts for an incredibly large portion of the average family's monthly budget. And what we can't afford to pay for with our own credit, Uncle Sam covers. Government spending over the past decade exceeded government revenues by about $3 trillion. And on top of this we have a mountain of corporate debt, which directly funds economic expansion. In short, we're paying for our expanding production with debt. We're not even coming close to covering it with money we earn today. Theoretically, it is impossible to do so. And unless we replace our assumptions about growth, we'll just continue to dig a bigger hole for ourselves.

Interestingly, of the four economic plans I mentioned at the beginning of this chapter, Patterson and Kim found through extensive surveys that the American public overwhelmingly favors Jack Kemp's return to supply-side economics. In other words, most Americans want to use government resources to spur an even greater expansion in our production base, in hope that we can somehow consume all that production and keep the economy growing. This is both madness and a sure-fire recipe for economic disaster.

The Problem of Profit

The preceding discussion of John Hobson's ideas hints at the underlying question of this chapter. *What makes the capitalist economy grow?* The answer is very simple: profit. Profit is of course the difference between what a company charges for its products and what it spends. If the company reinvests that excess to expand production capacity, we call it capital, and it is the pursuit of capital that makes the capitalist economy grow. And Hobson would tell us that it is this engine of growth itself that prevents a capitalist society from consuming all that it produces—unless it invests abroad or purchases on credit.

The lust for capital is what causes the gap between the haves and have-nots to widen. Most people are motivated by the desire to increase their wealth. Why not? I don't know many people who would rather be poor than rich. But those who own or control capital have leverage in this quest for wealth. They profit by keeping costs down while charging as much as the market will allow for their products. Their incentive, therefore, is to pay their employees as little as possible, and to keep for themselves as much as possible. The widening gap between rich and poor is simply evidence of this incentive.

So those who already own capital strive to increase that capital by reaping a profit. And this brings us to a question that perplexed worldly philosophers for centuries: *Where do profits come from?* Curiously, only three reasonable answers were ever put forward: one by Karl Marx, another by Joseph Schumpeter, and a third by Thorstein Veblen. Even the venerable Adam Smith wavered on this question between two possible answers.

For a more detailed examination of these theories, I recommend Robert Heilbroner's classic, *The Worldly Philosophers*, but let me briefly outline the three answers to this pivotal question. Marx would tell us that in capitalist economies, profits tend to disappear over time as market forces equalize wages and advantages. This was not an original insight. Adam Smith, David Ricardo, and John Stuart Mill had already pointed out the same thing. What Marx did was to create a model of capitalism to show where this phenomenon would lead and to explain how it worked.

Marx's model was not patterned after reality. It was a theoretically "perfect" capitalism. And what he concluded was that profit could exist in the capitalist system only when the capitalists stole it from the laborers. By paying them less than their actual value, capitalists were able to extract profit from their operations.

Marx's model is very involved and does have several gaping holes in it, and others have adequately exposed these, but Marx's ideas are significant because they do offer an explanation of where profit comes from.

To Joseph Schumpeter, profit was not stolen into existence, rather, it came honestly from innovation. He describes production and consumption as a circular flow that follows a regular and predictable course: people trading money and products with one another. So where do profits come from? They magically appear whenever the circular flow of production and consumption departs from its usual course. And when does this happen? Whenever an innovation enters the system. Whenever someone invents a new machine or new product, devises a new method of production, or improves quality, this disrupts the flow.

Innovation allows someone to take money out of the flow, either because quality has increased and people are willing to pay slightly more, or because production has become more efficient and the capitalist needn't pay as much to someone else, yet can temporarily charge the traditional price for a product. Profit, to Schumpeter, is a temporary glitch in the flow of production and consumption. Before long, everyone's quality will increase or their costs will decline as they learn the new method or purchase the new machinery. Then, as in Marx's model, profit is squeezed out of the system. Profit exists in Schumpeter's world only in a transient state. It is a temporary phenomenon, a constantly recurring temporary phenomenon, which explains the survival of the system.

Thorstein Veblen offers yet another view of profit. He saw "the economic process itself as being basically mechanical in character. Economic meant production, and production meant the machinelike meshing of society as it turned out goods. Such a social machine would need tenders, of course—technicians and engineers to make whatever adjustments were necessary to ensure the most efficient cooperation of the parts" (Heilbroner, 1986, 235). But, asked Veblen, where does the businessman fit in? The businessman, he concluded, was basically a saboteur of the system who extracted a profit by disrupting it.

The system itself saw no other end except making *goods*. The businessman, however, was interested only in making *money*. But "if the machine functioned well and fitted together smoothly, where would there be a place for a man whose only aim was profit? Ideally, there would be none. The machine was not concerned with values and profits; it ground out goods. . . . So the businessman achieved his end, not by working within the framework of the social machine, but by conspiring against it! His function was not to help make goods, but to cause breakdowns in the regular flow of output so that values would fluctuate and he could capitalize on the confusion to reap a profit" (ibid., 235-36).

And how did the businessman cause these breakdowns in the production machine? By creating the never-never-land of corporate finance. "On top of the machinelike dependability of the actual production apparatus," explains Heilbroner, "the businessman built a superstructure of credit, loans, and make-believe capitalizations. Below, society turned over in its mechanical routine; above, the structure of finance swayed and shifted. And as the financial counterpart to the real world teetered, opportunities for profit constantly appeared, disappeared, and reappeared" (ibid., 236).

Now, all three—Marx, Schumpeter, and Veblen—were partially right. They isolated direct causes of profit in individual businesses, but none of them carried the question to the next logical level and identified the underlying source of all profit (and all growth) in the capitalist economy.

It's easy to see where one company's profit comes from. Xerox, for instance, simply charges more for its copiers than it pays to produce them. The difference between what it brings in as revenues and spends as various expenses appears on its financial statements as profit. But if we look at the economy as a whole, how does it profit, or expand, each year? Where does growth come from? Well, directly, it comes from the surpluses of its specific parts and pieces. Individuals and corporations either reinvest their wages and profits in production capacity to expand our product base or spend them on old and new products to increase the overall level of consumption. Who can deny that the economy encompasses more goods and services than it did a decade ago? There are more cellular phones, more microwave dinners, more books about the economy, more consultants, more accountants, and more fast food outlets than there were last year. But this explanation—that the economy grows because of recurring profit in its individual parts and pieces—misses something important: *How is it that the sum of all businesses experiences more profit than loss in a given time period?*

As we trade money and products with one another, shouldn't profit and loss cancel each other out? In other words, in an economy where imports and exports balance (and therefore cancel each other out), shouldn't total business revenues exactly equal total business expenses? Some may point out that business revenue is made up of both expenditures by other businesses and consumer purchases. But where do consumers get the money to spend? From their wages, which are a business expense. Where, then, does the surplus come from? How do we solve this paradox? The answer is that, yes, indeed, total revenues and expenses should be equal—*unless the quantity of money in the system increases*. If new money enters the picture, then total revenues can in fact exceed total expenditures.

This, then, is how the economy expands. New money is introduced—primarily through a nifty bit of financial magic we might call borrowing money into existence—and this sustains economic growth. The new money permits capitalists to extract a profit from their operations (it also permits individuals and organizations to profit from financial speculation), and it allows revenues to exceed total expenses in any given period of time.

Our Outrageous Demand for Profits

It is important for us to make a distinction at this point. Infusing new money into the system doesn't *make* the economy grow. It merely makes growth possible. It supports and sustains growth.

Individual businesses still have to find a way to extract profit from the flow. And here we come full circle back to Marx and Schumpeter and Veblen—and to the fundamental problems with their solutions.

Capitalists can steal profits from employees by paying them less than they are worth, and this happens every day in the regular course of business. There are many underpaid individuals in organizational America—underpaid in the sense that they are unable to consume their share of overall production. Hobson's dilemma again. Why must this be? For the simple reason that if organizational America paid its employees enough so that they could purchase the exact amount of production they add to the economy, there would be, by definition, no profit, no excessive executive salaries and bonuses, and no dividends to stockholders. In order to make a profit, businesses must pay employees a diminishing portion of the system's total wealth, must prevent them from purchasing as much as they produce. The only way to keep this illogical system going, as discussed earlier, is for businesses to convince their employees to buy today's production with tomorrow's paycheck. But debt is merely a short-term solution. Over time, it is lethal, because if further reduces the ability of the working class to buy its fair share of production.

Schumpeter would tell us we can extract profit by introducing innovations into the system. The problem with this is that our economic health becomes dependent on continual innovation. We must perpetually make existing products obsolete by replacing them with newer versions; we must constantly improve quality, endlessly invent new products, and forever refine production processes so that we can make things less expensively. This constant obsolescence and the increase in available products, however, are filling our lives and our world with junk. I've been to the local landfill and have seen firsthand the mess created by our disposable society. But I also look around my house and can't believe all the things my family possesses, and how few of them we really need or use. And it's getting worse. As the economy grows, the total innovation needed to sustain growth multiplies, as does the waste in the system. This discussion, of course, dovetails with the environmental argument.

Finally, Veblen would tell us that profit is the result of financial manipulations by businessmen who actually sabotage the system. The problem with this source of profit is that it divorces the financial system from the apparatus of production and consumption and makes profit an end in itself. In Veblen's world, just as in Schumpeter's, most of the goods that clamor for our spare change (or remaining credit) are not an end in themselves, items that people actually need or that improve their lives. Most products sold in today's market are means to an end, and that end is profit. They were created, not because we need them or even want them, but so that someone could manipulate and confuse the productive machinery and extort a profit from the flow. Production has become a tool of finance, not the reverse.

"Twenty years ago," write Daly and Cobb, "the greatest power over the global economy may have been that of transnational corporations engaged in production. Today that power has shifted to institutions dealing with finance. Investment has come increasingly to mean the buying and selling of productive enterprises rather than their establishment or expansion" (Daly and Cobb, [1989] 1994, 436).

Financial markets, adds Hawken, "reduce acts of commerce, which always have significant impact on human and natural life, to mere finance, to a decimal, to basis points, to net present value. We are turning over the financing of the world, if we haven't already, to money lenders whose interests and incentives revolve around minute increments gained in the sale of abstracted financial instruments" (Hawken, 1993, 94). Indeed, financial manipulation has grown so prevalent that we now have what has been called a *paper economy*, or "the direct conversion of money into more money without reference to commodities even as an intermediate step" (Daly and Cobb, [1989] 1994, 410).

Finance as an end in itself is a scary thing. When money becomes the most-sought-after product, something is terribly wrong, for money is no product at all. Money is a tool, a pure fiction we use to ease the exchange of real products. John Stuart Mill described money as simply "a machine for doing quickly and commodiously, what would be done, though less quickly and commodiously, without it: and like many other kinds of machinery, it only exerts a distinct and independent influence of its own when it gets out of order" (Mill, [1848] 1886, 9).

Money in our day has indeed gotten out of order. It has become the most sought after commodity of all, able to expand exponentially without any reference at all to real economic growth or contraction. And because of this, an increasingly speculative currency market has arisen. The financial superstructure in our economy has lost touch almost completely with the actual production and consumption of goods and services. Consequently, the world economy is becoming what Willis Harman calls "one vast gambling casino." The ballooning derivatives market—a universe of side bets as far removed from Veblen's financial superstructure as the superstructure is removed from the real world—is the latest manifestation of speculation gone crazy.

To illustrate how out of control money is, consider that annual world trade exceeds $3 trillion. World financial flows, on the other hand, reach nearly $100 trillion per year. What this means, says Harman, is that less than 5 percent of the "funds sloshing around the globe" have anything whatever to do with "goods and services that enhance human life" (Harman, 1994). To put it mildly, both the world economy and the American economy are growing more and more distant from the real world in which people eat, sleep, live, work, die, and consume. The mitotic propagation of money has totally overwhelmed the direct, beneficial type of transactions in which people buy and sell products to better their lives.

In our out-of-control economy, we have too intense a demand for profit, especially profit derived from speculation. There is, however, a vast difference between money and real wealth. Money, which can be created out of thin air, can also grow endlessly. The real, physical economy, on the other hand, is bound by equally real, physical limits. In essence, much of the growth we have seen in recent years has been nothing more than a clever mirage. But growth we must have, even if it is illusory growth, because without growth, capitalism dies.

Capitalism, no matter whose model you like, requires a constantly expanding market, requires that luxuries become necessities, that we constantly improve and replace products in an endless upward spiral, that we extract an increasing amount of profit, and that we infuse new money regularly into the economic flow. Everyone agrees on this. These are the assumptions behind everyone's solutions. No one questions the insanity of the system at its most fundamental levels.

But is the system never satiated? Must we forever buy and sell an increasing number of products, introduce new luxuries, transform old luxuries into necessities, make technologies obsolete at an accelerating rate, shop till we drop, worlds without end? The answer is apparently yes. The capitalist economy must grow. The alternative is, well, unthinkable. "When the monster stops growing," explain the owner men in Steinbeck's

Grapes of Wrath, "it dies. It can't stay one size." Growth is the most fundamental assumption of capitalism. For without growth there *is* no capitalism, because there is no profit, no surplus to turn into capital.

Burning Muscle

The growth assumption worked well for many years. The supply of goods and services has grown and grown and grown, and our technological progress has been impressive. But what we never asked ourselves was where this line of thinking would take us. Is our path a never-ending upward spiral, or does it end somewhere, and, if it does, where does it end and how? I suggest that we are now beginning to learn the answers to those questions—some of them are economic, some environmental. Our economy is spiraling out of control, the slope is steepening, and to move forward we must accelerate our climb—we must reach the next level more rapidly, at greater velocity, or we won't have the momentum to carry us to the next, even higher and steeper level.

This is why we are experiencing such an incredible demand for profits in our economy, why companies are so glued to the short-term bottom line. If they don't have the capital to jump right now to the next step, which very often is dictated by new waves of technology that are hitting the shore with increasing frequency, they will be left behind—forever. They will never make the next step.

Aside from the disconcerting fact that intense competitive pressures are leaving numerous businesses in the dust, even more ominous is the fact that the economy also is abandoning millions of individuals. The economy, says Edward O. Welles, "has grown more Darwinian. The highly skilled prosper. The skilled survive. The unskilled fall prey to change" (Welles,

1994, 98). Soon only the most educated and productive workers will occupy high-paying jobs. What will happen to the rest? How will they find enough cash to hold up their end of the equation, consumption, while the efficient and highly capitalized few quicken their already frenzied pace of production?

Unfortunately, the economy is not a machine that we can control scientifically. Rather, it exhibits the characteristics of a living system, and all living systems are, by nature, self-limiting. They grow normally to a certain point, after which they plateau and eventually decline. And the faster living systems grow, the sooner they reach their natural limits. If we try to push them past those limits, we damage them. And we have definitely pushed the economy past its natural confines.

Like a marathon runner at the end of the race, we're no longer burning fat reserves; we're burning muscle. Specifically, we're burning out viable businesses and we're burning up the middle class, creating a two-tiered society, and the lower tier is increasingly incapable of consuming all the products the upper tier is busily creating with its overabundance of capital.

Living Beyond Our Means

One reason we have managed, on the whole, to stay on the steep upward growth spiral without collapsing is that we are extracting our natural resources and transforming them into products at an ever-increasing rate. We are using up many renewable resources faster than we can replenish them. And we are depleting our nonrenewable resources more rapidly than ever. In essence, the world economy is living beyond its collective means. If we look at the global economy as a business, it is headed for financial ruin. As Paul Hawken reminds us, "No business in the world can long survive on its capital reserves. Every businessperson understands this, yet many ignore the fact that this same principle applies equally to energy and the environment" (Hawken, 1993, 181). Our collective human business, the world economy, is not living on its current energy income, but on its capital reserves. Any business that pursues this strategy will be bankrupt as soon as the capital runs out.

The economy has reached and exceeded its natural limits, but we fail to admit it. We try to force it to grow, and so it has become like an athlete on steroids: in many ways it is inhumanly strong and agile, but because the growth is artificially induced, its long-term well-being is compromised, it is developing severe emotional irregularities, and it is even beginning to acquire certain freak characteristics. It is definitely not what you would term healthy.

The economy has reached a point at which the old theories no longer work. Our accepted explanations of economic phenomena are now the equivalent of Newtonian physics. They worked well up to a point, but are now inadequate. What we need is a new economic theory, based on different, sounder assumptions. We need an economy that can provide for our needs without being dependent on perpetual growth.

Nothing in the modern workplace, and very little in society at large, encourages us to take our time, or be satisfied with what we have. We're being presented instead with a future where we will have to work harder, but have even less leisure time than we do today, if we are going to maintain our way of life. . . . We are speeding up our lives and working harder in a futile attempt to buy the time to slow down and enjoy it.

—Paul Hawken,
The Ecology of Commerce

4

When Speed Looks Like Growth

❧

Perhaps the most ubiquitous prescription for healing modern capitalism's ills is *productivity*. Some have called it a cure-all. According to the current economic dogma, it is the grand key to growth in our economy. So, unless we begin to question the growth imperative, economic expansion is the highway we must travel, and productivity is the vehicle that will take us to whatever fate lies at the end of the road.

And here we come to a paradox in economic America. If productivity is such a powerful panacea, and if our productivity is indeed increasing, then why haven't we seen its effects in our everyday lives? Why do we have to keep working harder and harder just to stay where we are? For most Americans, life in today's economy is like running up a down escalator. We have become more productive and have applied new technology as if it were a literal scientific savior, but real wages have stagnated, even retreated over the past twenty-five years.

Where Does Our Increased Productivity Go?

One thing is certain: the need for increased productivity today is *not* created by the expanding wants of the average American citizen. Yes, we may be the "want it all now" generation, but our wants, if anything, have been tempered by the sobering reality that we can afford much less per hour worked than we could twenty years ago—*in spite of our increased productivity.*

The average worker today—who, we are told, is much more productive than workers of twenty years ago—earns less in real wages than the average worker received in the early 1970s. Granted, we can buy high-tech wonders like laptop computers, microwave ovens, and CD players that our parents would never have dreamed of either needing or wanting, but the staples—housing, food (if you add in government subsidies), health care, and transportation—are relatively much more expensive now than they were twenty years ago. Sure, I can afford a cellular telephone and cable TV, but a house is much less affordable for me than it was for my parents. Our rising productivity, ironically, gets us less of the things we really need with each passing year and yet puts increasing pressure on us to purchase things we don't really need.

I would argue that in our society the cost of increasing productivity has reached the point at which it seriously outweighs the benefits. Who, to put it bluntly, profits from my increased productivity? I don't. Not if my name is Average Joe American. Average Joe has been working harder and harder for the past twenty years and is relatively worse off. The economic treadmill has speeded up, and Joe has to run faster and faster just to stay in one place. This being the case, we must ask where this ever-increasing productivity goes? Who, specifically is benefiting from Joe's increased productivity? There are at least three relevant answers.

The first and perhaps most significant item that eats up Joe's productivity increases is the *peripheral support structure* that has been erected for the sole purpose of holding up the sagging weight of capitalism-run-amok. Many of my neighbors, to use a close-to-home example, aren't directly involved in producing an actual product, something tangible like a refrigerator or rutabaga or car tire—or even something less tangible but equally useful like a haircut or dental examination or history lesson.

We employ millions of people in our economy who sell insurance, shuffle paper, count money, compile statistics, create junk mail, process information, file things, sue other people, manage political "images," rearrange corporate assets, collect taxes, conduct meaningless research, play the market, dream up deceptive advertisements, supervise people who are capable of supervising themselves, invest other people's money, and so on. These jobs are not only proliferating, but they also create a drag on productivity, because they are not materially involved in creating tangible products. Most peripheral service jobs cannot be made more productive—not in any significant sense—by either increased worker diligence or technological improvement. How many personal-claim lawsuits or divorces, for instance, can one lawyer handle in a given month? How many more audits can an IRS agent perform this year than last year? How does a corporate spin doctor increase his productivity?

As new technology displaces workers who actually produce tangible products (because actual production jobs are the most conducive to technology-related productivity improvement), these workers find jobs mainly in the expanding service sector. And as the service sector becomes ever larger, it dilutes the productivity increases of those who are producing tangible goods.

The second black hole into which Joe's increased productivity disappears is *the widening gap between the rich and the poor* (and, we might add, between the rich and those in the middle). According to a 1994 report by President Clinton's Commission on the Future of Worker-Management Relations, the top 10 percent of American workers earn salaries an average of 5.63 times greater than wages paid to workers in the bottom 10 percent, a range that is "by far the widest" of all industrialized countries. We are creating a "two-tier" wage structure, which siphons off Joe's productivity increases and puts them into someone else's bank account. (See Sawyer, 1994.)

Besides the traditional accumulation of capital by the affluent and the redistribution of wealth—from poor to rich—through the presence of massive debt in the system, the capitalist and executive class is simply taking more of Joe's productivity increases to line its own pockets than it did in the past. It used to be that a bigger portion of Joe's increased output was invested back into the company. Nowadays, however, the salaries and bonuses and incentives of owners and top executives have gone through the ceiling. And most, if not all, of this executive pay, comes out of Joe's increased output.

The third hungry mouth that devours Joe's increased productivity is *debt*—corporate, trade, and national. The binge of mergers and acquisitions, LBOs and hostile takeovers during the 1980s left corporate America with a nasty hangover. "Large companies," says Robert Reich, "are spending upwards of 30 percent of cash flow in interest on borrowing that has been used to defend against potential takeovers or to mount takeovers themselves" (Reich, 1992, 15). The debt we created at this extended office party had two effects. It soaked up loan money that could have been used to strengthen small businesses; it also forced companies to lay off thousands of workers and require those who escaped the ax to increase their efficiency. This increased productivity is mainly used to pay off principal and interest—and makes the lenders of money wealthier than ever.

On the national level, productivity continues to rise, but only at a rate of about 1 percent per year (averaged over the past 15 years). The national debt, on the other hand, has increased since 1977 at an annual rate of about 12.5 percent. To put this in a different perspective, our interest payments on the national debt in 1992 of $292 billion exceeded that year's annual increase in GNP by $25 billion. In essence, our increased output is not quite enough to pay the interest on the national debt. And what about consumer, corporate, and trade debt? Even though we steadily increase our productivity, we're losing ground. No wonder Average Joe is so frustrated.

Is Productivity Improvement Really a Panacea?

The upshot of all this is that our current economic predicament is taking a tremendous toll on the average American. To appease our insatiable demand for growth, Joe must work harder and harder, or else be replaced by either new technology that can work more efficiently or foreign labor that can work more cheaply. If he is displaced, he usually winds up in a lower-paying service-sector job, or two or three jobs, and must work horrendous hours just to pay the bills. The result is a frantic lifestyle in which he runs faster and faster and yet falls further and further behind. The economy's demands are consuming his life.

Why do we feel we must increase our productivity to maintain economic health? Primarily because of our belief that this is what improves our standard of living and makes the economy grow. But is it possible that we are barking up the wrong tree? Is it possible that expanding productivity has no direct correlation to economic health? Our frantic push to increase productivity is not improving our economic lot. Is it possible that our problems stem from other causes? Is it conceivable that our constricting "productivity or bust" approach, may actually be *counterproductive?*

Growth or Speed?

The need for the economy to grow is what drives our current productivity craze, but the very idea that increasing productivity will cause the economy to expand may be more fiction than fact. This statement is absurd if you believe conventional wisdom, but conventional wisdom is what I'm questioning in this book. Let's look closely, then, at what happens when we increase productivity in an economy.

The problem with conventional wisdom lies in our understanding of what productivity actually does. Productivity on a national level is a concept that gets lost in the fog of nebulous and largely useless statistics. But at the level of the individual worker, productivity means simply producing more units of a particular product in a fixed time period. We can express productivity as a ratio—output divided by input. We generally define output as units of product created; the input we usually choose to measure is labor hours, although this is an admittedly incomplete and sometimes misleading measuring stick.

Once we define exactly what we mean by productivity, there are two distinct ways of viewing productivity increases. One way is to focus on the numerator in the ratio: *In an average hour the worker produces 12 units of product this month, compared to 10 units last month.* The other way of looking at productivity increases, which is just as valid, is to emphasize the denominator: *It takes the worker an average of 50 minutes to produce 10 units of product this month, compared with 60 minutes last month.* The first approach defines increased productivity in terms of *more* product. The second defines it in terms of *faster* production. Growth versus speed.

The pivotal question, however, is: *Does increased productivity add real wealth to the system?* And the answer is both yes and no, depending on which way you look at it. In the traditional sense, increasing productivity enlarges the quantity of goods available for our use and consumption, and therefore we might say that it adds wealth to the economy. But real wealth (not the money that symbolizes it) is perishable. We can't easily store it, because it either rots or becomes obsolete. Consequently, we must do one of three things with it: use it up, consume it, or convert it into debt by trading it to others for a share of their future production. Since real wealth is perishable, if we do not consume it, use it up, or trade it to someone else who can use it, it becomes valueless. It is expedient, therefore, that we purchase all the goods we produce with our expanding productivity. Consumption must keep up with production. And this brings us to the question of speed.

If the time it takes us to produce a given quantity of goods steadily decreases, then we must also consume those goods more rapidly. Everything speeds up. In this sense, productivity does not make us wealthier as a society. We simply produce and consume at a faster pace. *There is not really more wealth in the system. It merely appears so, because money and products change hands faster.*

Whichever way you look at it, increasing productivity enables capitalists to put their extracted excess to use more frequently. We might say it increases turnover. There are indeed more products in the system during a fixed time period and, in this sense, rising productivity does increase wealth. But we also consume those products at an accelerated pace—our wealth perishes more rapidly. In other words, escalating productivity simply creates a convincing illusion of greater wealth, to say nothing of a more hectic lifestyle.

The problem with this method of achieving economic growth is that in a very fundamental way it is not growth at all. *It is merely speed that looks like growth.* In a very real sense, our spiral of productivity-driven economic growth is not actually expanding—it is simply turning faster and faster, and the faster it turns, the steeper the slope gets. The dilemma we face with a system addicted to this type of "growth" is that once you reach a high level of productivity, each additional increase becomes more difficult, even as those increases become more critical in maintaining upward momentum. It's easy for me to cut three minutes off my time if I run a twenty-minute mile. But if I run a four-minute mile, each second I can cut off my time comes at a tremendous effort.

To repeat a metaphor from the previous chapter, we could say that our productivity-driven economy is cancerous. Cancer can be defined simply as uncontrolled cellular growth. Cancer cells, if you will, are tremendously productive cells. They have speeded up natural processes to the point where they have mutated and lost their ability to function usefully. So instead of adding to the health of the body, they become destructive by growing in an uncontrolled manner and depriving normal cells of nutrients.

The Technological Trap

Ever-increasing productivity is possible only in a climate of continually advancing technology. Because of this fact, our present assumptions leave us no choice but to encourage technology to expand as fast as possible. Indeed, the new thinking regarding today's hypercompetitive global marketplace is that if we are to flourish, we need to achieve the impossible—somehow to come up with endless, brilliant, cheap innovation. If we don't constantly reach new levels of innovation, we get left behind—as individuals, as companies, as a nation. Contrary to what the experts suggest, however, the question is not, "How can we begin to function at these levels?" but rather, "How long can we pursue this insanity before we self-destruct?"

A consumer society, driven by the demands of an ever-expanding technology, is inherently self-destructive. The problem is that as new technologies replace old ones at an accelerating pace, few consumers or companies can keep up. Only the biggest and wealthiest survive, which results in the concentrating of both power and capital in society.

Technology is such an enticing path to step onto. On the surface, it offers us the solutions to all our problems. New technology gives us an advantage in the marketplace, allows us either to produce less expensively or to charge more for newer, higher-quality products, and enables us to accumulate more capital than our competitors. This is a short-term view, though. To stay ahead in the game, or even to stay in the game, we must invest in ever-newer technology, which, as competition intensifies, becomes more frequent and more expensive.

Consider the computer industry as an example. "Any semiconductor maker aspiring to hold or gain market share," says Charles Ferguson, "must spend enormous sums of money. Current technology requires, on average, $200 million to $1 billion for each generation of process development, $250 million to $400 million for each factory, and $10 million to $100 million for each major device design" (Ferguson, 1990, 55-56). And with each new generation (approximately every four years), the R&D and capital-investment requirements double. This is not a game any small or medium-sized company can join. Only the multi-billion-dollar corporations can play. In industries such as this, companies are not merely developing technology to further their own ends; technology is actually driving companies in an insanely steep spiral of repeated investment, production, and obsolescence. Not many companies can survive long in this deadly race, and not many consumers can afford the increasing frequency of obsolescence.

Ironically, corporate America has always operated on the assumption that ever-advancing technology is the way out of the mess, rather than the way in. Organizational America, in myopic devotion to its own self-interest, never has understood that unbridled technology is like cocaine. At first it gives you a sense of euphoria and power, a befuddled optimism that you can accomplish anything. But you quickly become addicted to it and, as time passes, you find you need larger and larger doses just to keep functioning at normal levels. It soon becomes a way of life. You live for the drug. It affects your health and interferes with your everyday obligations, and eventually you can't afford it, so you steal (from future generations) or go into debt to get another fix. It soon controls your life, and it will kill you unless you can throw off its chains.

Unbridled technology is not a panacea for society's ills. It is not even a harmless short-term thrill. It is a parasite—it thrives and procreates by consuming its host, because the host is never capable of sustaining both itself and the parasite. Soon the parasite becomes too large and powerful and burdensome. For the host will never be composed of only high-tech, high-paid elements. Society's inherent mix of mental and manual, high-tech and low-tech members establishes a natural limit to the practical expansion of technology.

If we do not carefully control technology's expansion, it replaces high-paid low-tech workers with low-cost automated processes, pushes those formerly high-paid production workers into low-paying service-sector jobs, shifts wealth from displaced workers to those who own or control the technology, and forces the lower economic levels of society to go into debt to maintain the lifestyle they are accustomed to. Yes, they may have a few more high-tech possessions, which they are able to own because automation has made them more affordable, but life in general, especially big-ticket items like cars and houses and medical care, become so expensive that fewer and fewer people can afford them. We wind up with many workers in low-paying service sector jobs and significantly fewer in high-wage, low-tech jobs; the average income drops; and the only way we can maintain an increasingly expensive standard of living is to borrow it from our children and grandchildren.

Unless we change our assumptions regarding growth and productivity, there will always be pressure to find newer, cheaper, more brilliant innovations. And the pressure will multiply over time. The ideology of progress and growth insists on faster and faster innovation in a never-ending, ever-expanding spiral of production and consumption. And that spiral is growing steeper today in nearly every industry. But where is this spiral leading us? Are we really moving upward and outward, or are we actually traveling in tighter and tighter circles—like water in a bathtub—before we finally go down the drain?

Can we afford this materialistic ideology? I'm talking real dollars and cents here. You don't have to be an economist to realize that the suffocating spiral of newer and faster innovation cannot continue forever. Even if we had inexhaustible economic resources, we would eventually bump up against very real physical limits. All the technology in the world can make human beings work only so fast. But we'll never hit the physical limits, because we're already hitting economic limits. Our increasing productivity is vanishing into the void even as it decreases our overall purchasing power. It isn't really making our lives better, not in the comprehensive sense. Although we are working faster and faster, our standard of living and real wages are declining. We cannot afford the demands of ever-accelerating productivity, for it is quickly exhausting and bankrupting us, individually and collectively.

The Technological Assumption

A troubling consequence of our single-minded dedication to increasing productivity is that technology, which can be a valuable tool to better our individual and collective lives, has instead become merely an instrument to make individual businesses and the larger economy grow. Businesses do not develop and invest in new technologies to better society. That may happen by luck or chance, but the truth is that businesses develop technologies for the express purpose of becoming more competitive, capturing market share, and increasing their profits.

This prostituting of technology leads to some unfortunate end results, partly because we have come to assume a connection between technology and quality of life that, in fact, does not exist. This assumption, which I have dubbed *the technological assumption,* is the largely unspoken but pervasive belief that quality of life is to be measured solely in technological terms. In other words, *society advances only as technology advances.* Although few would deny that civilization is more than material comforts, and that quality of life has spiritual dimensions, the technological assumption is nonetheless so prevalent (we are constantly immersed in its advertising) that the demands of an ever-expanding technology dictate both the shape and pace of our lives.

Because of this pervasive influence, we simply find ourselves measuring society's progress in terms of comfort and gadgets and technological wonders—space shuttles, CAT scanners, high-definition TVs, aerodynamic automobiles, laptop computers, laser printers, cordless telephones, fax machines, CD players, microwave ovens—and yet in so many ways these measuring sticks of material progress have contributed to an ongoing societal decadence.

Television, for example, was supposed to be (and still might become) a great educational and informational tool, and yet we are now finding that a generation glued to the tube knows so little about the world it lives in that its ignorance frightens us. If you measure its impact by what most Americans watch on a weekly basis, television has not broadened our horizons. Rather, it has captivated and tranquilized our minds to the extent that we cannot think for ourselves. We simply listen and believe. And sometimes we mimic—and that's when it gets scary. The fault lies not with the technology itself, of course, but with our use of it, and that use is effectively orchestrated by big business, which has its own agenda.

Profit-driven technology has in many ways made our lives easier, perhaps it has even inadvertently made them *better* in some ways, but has it made them *good*? Such conveniences as fax machines, personal computers, microwave ovens, and cellular telephones have enabled us to hurry faster, but have they really improved the quality of our lives? It might be argued they have done just the opposite.

Facsimile machines have taken away even the pretense that some aspects of business are not urgent. Now overnight mail is too slow. Everything has to be done now, now, now. We've lost the ability to be patient. As one businessman put it, nowadays people call you on the phone to tell you your fax line's busy.

What about the computer? Oh, I agree, it has made life less tedious—I would have a hard time without mine, in fact—but I have taught college students who cannot write an intelligible sentence because the word processor now checks their spelling and their grammar, and they apparently assume that it can also think for them. They do not realize that writing is the finest exercise to develop clear thinking. Many of these same students are calculator-bound and can't do simple arithmetic in their brains. An extreme case was the university senior who reduced a problem on an exam to $2x = 100$ and then couldn't arrive at the value of x without his calculator.

On a much higher plane, computers are opening the doors to perplexing moral questions in such areas as nuclear physics, medicine, and biotechnology. We are walking through those doors eagerly, without asking whether or not those doors should be opened at all, and without accepting the responsibility for the potential consequences of our steps. Technology's forward march cannot be denied. If it *can* be done, it *should* be done, especially if there's a profit in it.

And we call this civilization? Social progress? Yes, we call it that. For we've fully indoctrinated ourselves in scientific capitalism's (and communism's) *a priori* equation: technological advance = societal progress. The problem with this equation is one that General Omar Bradley recognized decades ago: "Our knowledge of science has clearly outstripped our capacity to control it. . . . The world has achieved brilliance without wisdom, power without conscience. Ours is a world of nuclear giants and ethical infants."

The problem is not in developing new technology that might be of benefit to mankind. Of course we can and should do this. The real problem lies in making technology work for us, rather than allowing ourselves to be driven in undesirable directions by technology's tendency toward rapid and endless proliferation. "[Jacques Ellul's] point," say William Scott and David Hart, "was that although individuals can control single machines, the network of machines and organizations is beyond them: 'If man can claim to be the master of a machine, and even of every machine considered successively, can he claim to be the master of the technological whole of which each machine is a part?' It is the whole interlocking network of machines that is the problem. But who, specifically, has the responsibility to control the whole? Indeed, who has the capacity to even understand the whole, let alone control it?" (Scott and Hart, 1989, 28-29)

We are developing new technology without either the moral sense or the social vision to use it correctly and control its proliferation. Consequently, it is using us, shaping us because we refuse to shape it. The technological economy is in control, and we do its bidding, believing its claim that science, science, and more science are the three magic keys to human progress and happiness.

The Crisis of the Postindustrial Society

Let me put today's high-tech economy in some kind of historical context. In the early 1800s, 90 percent of the workforce was involved in agriculture. Farming wasn't merely the occupation of choice—it was the occupation of necessity. It simply took nine out of every ten workers to provide food for society. But increased productivity (mainly due to technology) changed all that. Technological advancements in agriculture made farmers more efficient—in two ways. The farmer could accomplish more with his time, and he could also get a better yield per acre. This has continued now for nearly two centuries. By 1940 one farm worker could supply ten nonfarmers with food. By 1980 those ten had increased to seventy-five, and by 1990 less than 2 percent of the total workforce labored in agriculture. The only downside to all this progress was that it eliminated the need for so many agricultural laborers.

This wasn't an economic problem, however, for technological advances not only caused more bushels per farmer, they also created numerous new factory jobs. Displaced farm help simply moved to the cities and took jobs in manufacturing facilities. This shift represented a significant change in society—the first major change in centuries, in fact.

This, however, was only the beginning. Over the past century technology has worked a similar transformation in manufacturing. Technological innovations have made factory workers increasingly productive. Consequently, we have need today for far fewer blue-collar workers than ever before. And the recent push to become competitive with foreign producers has only quickened the pace of job reduction for both manufacturing and support personnel.

The only problem is that most displaced manufacturing workers have no comparable-paying jobs to move into, as did their predecessors in agriculture. And our dilemma today isn't limited to manufacturing. In an attempt to become increasingly competitive, nearly every industry that produces a consumable product is downsizing. The bottom line is that increased productivity is creating an economy that requires fewer and fewer workers of all sorts to produce the goods and services we need and want. And both the competitive nature of our industries and recent technological trends indicate that productivity will continue to increase.

According to a *Fortune* magazine report in August 1992 ("Job Drought"), the number of full-time workers in the United States increased by 13.6 million between 1979 and 1989, but the median weekly wage of those workers (in 1989 dollars) dropped from $409.13 to $398.88. The reason for this wage decrease was the nature of the new jobs. While manufacturing shed some 675,000 jobs, most of them high-paying, 5 million of the 13.6

million new full-time jobs (almost all in services) paid less than $250 per week, $13,000 per year—below the poverty level for a family of four. More than 1.6 million of these new low-paying jobs were in restaurants, stockrooms, and retail sales (in other words, support functions for consumer-oriented rather than producer-oriented enterprises).

As a workforce, we have moved away from making things and toward merely buying and selling things. Because producing the items we need requires fewer and fewer workers, we have become a consumer society, the marketplace where the rest of the world can sell its wares. but what happens when we need only 10 or 20 percent of the population to manufacture the products we need and want? What do the rest of us do? Do we get up each morning, as William Abernathy once suggested, and press each other's pants? It might be argued that this is exactly what we are doing. A nation of superfluous service workers is not an economically healthy nation, and never can be. This is the dilemma of the postindustrial society.

The crux of the issue is that increased productivity, aimed at making companies competitive (and profitable), is inadvertently creating a greater division between the haves and have-nots and is therefore diluting our ability to consume all that we produce, unless we purchase on credit. Capitalism's solution to the dilemma of a shrinking manufacturing workforce is to introduce new products—primarily services—at an accelerating pace (to perpetually create new jobs to replace the ones we have eliminated). This curbs unemployment (though not misemployment), pressures us to consume more than ever before, and keeps the wheels of capitalism spinning, but how long can we sustain this expanding spiral of debt-driven economic activity without seeing the whole system collapse? An economy built on an expanding foundation of superfluous products and expendable workers cannot endure forever. Technology-driven productivity improvement is fast creating a society in which the vast majority of us must find work in nonproductive activities.

J. W. Smith points out that "when labor is cut from a production process [through the efficiency of technology], the share of production once claimed by this labor is then claimed by the owners of capital" (Smith, 1993-1994, 18). The rich get richer, and the poor get poorer, and the displaced laborer must find employment in nonproductive work. Because of the social rule "no work, no pay," nonproductive work will continue to expand as our need for production workers shrinks. Nonproductive work, however, does create two very real products: busywork, which is nothing more than making someone jump through an economic hoop to get a share of society's total income, and advertising, which is essential in the art of creating a need for superfluous products.

Smith estimates that there are more than "80 million people who are either unemployed or employed nonproductively" (ibid., 21). If we divided up the productive work equally, he adds, we would need to work only 2.3 days a week. "And since only unnecessary work would be eliminated, there would be no drop in our standard of living" (ibid.). Indeed, imagine all the desirable, society-enhancing things we might accomplish in our spare time, if we were simply to eliminate all the nonproductive jobs that our "no work, no pay" social philosophy necessitates.

Smith's ideas are intriguing, and they would result in a more equal and sane society, but they don't even address the issues of limitless growth and technology-driven productivity. To effectively rein in these out-of-control economic engines, we must also strive for fundamental philosophical and structural change.

Any way you slice it, our current assumptions and the solutions that spring from them make no sense at all, which is why

I've titled this book *Economic Insanity*, an apt description of our present predicament. But if the capitalist answer is not the right one, which direction are we to turn? To my knowledge there are only three other possible solutions:

1. Establish a pervasive welfare system to support the 80 or 90 percent of workers who are idle, so that they can consume their share of our increasing production.

2. Return to a more primitive technological state, which would reduce our productivity and increase the demand for low-tech workers.

3. Rethink the basic assumptions of capitalism, including endless growth, self-interested competition, nonproductive work, and our current system of unlimited capital ownership (which lies at the heart of both our increasing economic inequality and the compulsive drive to innovate workers out of their jobs).

Option 1 offers little if any hope. We've been moving in that direction for long enough now that we can read the writing on the wall. Option 2 is both undesirable and probably impossible. Only the third alternative makes any sense, and it is this alternative that I will explore and attempt to justify in the remainder of this book.

The current system is reaching the end of its useful life. It is creating too great a gap between the haves and have-nots and is based on the illogical premise that growth equals health. As with any living organism, though, this premise is valid only to a certain point. Beyond that point, growth is destructive, and several current indicators suggest that we have indeed reached that point. Consequently, we have but two choices. We can either stand by and watch an out-of-control economy devour our future, or we can replace it with a system that makes more sense for the long term.

Often there is one pay system for executives, the intent of which is to pay them as much as possible. There are other pay systems for managers and core workers. The intent of these is to keep labor costs as low as possible. . . . It is this class distinction that results in the incongruence of massive layoffs and record profits and executive bonuses all in the same year.

—Peter Block,
Stewardship

5

Of Course the Rich
Are Getting Richer

Though capitalists are also consumers, a distinct class difference divides the two groups. That distinction is revealed in the quotation from Peter Block on the opposite page. A good definition of what it means to be a capitalist is simply that a capitalist is paid as much as possible. Why? Because capitalists control capital, and it is capital that produces income. These people pay themselves as much as possible so that they can accumulate more capital—not to spend on consumer items, but primarily to reinvest in productive capacity, so that they can become even more wealthy and control an even larger piece of the productive pie.

Noncapitalists, by contrast, do not control capital, even when they invest their modest savings in stocks or bonds. Noncapitalists, because they do not control capital, are paid as little as possible (so that the capitalists can minimize costs and maximize profits). What they take home in wages is called *disposable income*. Why? Because they are supposed to dispose of it through consuming the products they produce. They are not supposed to become more wealthy. As Galbraith points out, their role in the economy is to consume.

The end result of this class division is an ever-widening monetary gap between the capitalists and the consumers. This is not a political phenomenon, nor is it the result of an uncompetitive or misfiring economy. It is simply the logical consequence of the capitalist system. Quite frequently I read articles in the newspaper expressing dismay over the fact that the rich are still getting richer and the poor relatively poorer. The articles always cite the most recent statistics, and the writers are invariably aghast over this continuing trend.

This is an irrational reaction, however, for capitalism is designed at its most fundamental levels to create increasing inequality. Somewhere, I suppose, many of us got the idea that capitalism and equality are compatible. Our reasoning must go something like this: since egalitarianism is part of the American Dream, then American capitalism should produce greater equality. This reasoning may be comfortable, but it is also defective. Which mechanism in the capitalist machine, I would ask, is supposed to equalize wealth? There is none.

Capitalism is genetically predisposed to shift relative wealth from the poor to the rich, or, if you prefer, from the unpropertied to the propertied. It's simply the nature of the beast. We can't expect it to act other than it is designed to act. Let's look at this idea more closely.

The "Leak-Through" Theory

I don't pretend to know who first came up with the notorious "trickle-down" theory. The term itself can be traced to about

1954, although the concept is at least old enough that William Jennings Bryan railed against it a century ago. Said the Great Commoner: "There are those who believe that if you will legislate to make the well-to-do prosperous, their prosperity will leak through on those below" (Will, 1994, 6). Bryan's "leak-through" theory is basically the same as today's trickle-down theory, which suggests that financial benefits given to the rich will filter on down to lower economic levels. This may be true, but there is nothing in the trickle-down theory to suggest that the lower levels of society will actually increase their *relative* wealth, and it is relative wealth that we're talking about here.

When capitalism creates new wealth, greater economic equality can result only if the capitalist class passes on more wealth *per capita* than it retains. When has this ever happened? Even the most rabid, bleeding-heart, Robin Hood liberal would never dream of taking so much from the rich that the poor actually gain more wealth *per capita* than their elite counterparts.

If the poorest 20 percent of Americans get a trickle (or leak) of wealth, we can be sure that the rich are receiving a flood. We've been told that a rising tide lifts all boats, but today's society can become more equal only if the rubber rafts and dinghies rise faster than the yachts and cruise ships. Unfortunately, though, the old "rising tide" maxim doesn't hold water— because some of our individual boats don't either. The system has punched holes in our hulls, and no matter how high the tide, we're still going to sink.

There was a time when the poorest levels of society were indeed receiving that infamous trickle of real wealth. They may have been falling further behind the rich, but in real terms they were able to improve their living standard. In recent years, however, both the poor and those in the middle have not only fallen further behind the rich, they have actually moved backwards in terms of real wealth. According to Robert Reich, between 1977 and 1989 "the average after-tax incomes of American families in the bottom fifth of the income ladder fell some 9 percent, the next fifth grew 6.5 percent poorer, and the middle fifth about 4.5 percent poorer. Only the top fifth was spared. In fact, the higher reaches of the top fifth were not only spared, their incomes soared. The incomes of those in the top 1 percent actually doubled" (Reich, 1992, 15).

Reich attributes this growing gap, particularly the downward movement of the lower and middle levels, to the loss of manufacturing jobs. Between 1989 and November 1992, he says, 1.3 million manufacturing jobs were lost in the United States. Most of these workers were forced into service jobs that paid only one-half to two-thirds of typical manufacturing wages.

This is trickle-down economics of the 1990s. Economic gains are defying gravity and trickling up. The lower levels are losing ground, not just in a relative sense, but in a very real sense.

Three Types of Workers

The loss in manufacturing jobs is the direct result of new technology that displaces labor and cheap foreign competition that persuades executives to move manufacturing facilities abroad. The rise of the global economy has created, among other effects, a sharp division between various types of labor.

In his book *The Work of Nations*, Reich identifies three separate categories of American workers that are emerging with the global economy: *routine producers*, *in-person servers*, and *symbolic analysts*. "No longer are Americans rising or falling together, as if in one large national boat. We are, increasingly, in different, smaller boats" (Reich, 1991, 171). Of the three types of boats listed above, only the third is rising with the economic tide.

Let's look briefly at these three groups and how they are faring.

Routine producers are those who perform repetitive tasks in the production of goods. This group includes not only blue-collar manufacturing workers, but also employees involved in white-collar or high-tech work. Data processors and programmers who devise routine coding for computer software come to mind. *In-person servers* may also perform routine work, but their services must be provided person-to-person. Retail sales workers, waiters and waitresses, custodians, cashiers, house cleaners, hospital attendants, taxi drivers, secretaries, auto mechanics, flight attendants, and security guards are typical of this category. *Symbolic analysts*, by contrast, engage in problem-identifying, problem-solving, decision-making, or strategy-brokering activities. These workers may be researchers, scientists, designers, engineers, public relations specialists, investment bankers, lawyers, consultants, systems analysts, advertising executives, film editors, art directors, architects, musicians, publishers, television producers, university professors, or seminar presenters, to list just a few.

As discussed in the previous chapter, routine production jobs are being lost continually to both foreign competition and technological advances. The thirty-five hours it took auto workers to assemble a car in 1977, for instance, has now been reduced to eight. Nippon Steel and Inland Steel built a cold-rolling mill near Gary, Indiana, in the late 1980s that cut the time to produce a coil of steel from twelve days to about one hour (ibid., 214). The masses of workers displaced by technology and those entering the job market who are not qualified for symbolic-analytical work must increasingly compete for low-paying in-person service jobs. There are plenty of these, but intense competition keeps wages low.

The only jobs that show great promise for the future involve data analysis and the manipulation of symbols. Great demand exists in the global economy for scientific researchers, management consultants, advertisers, architects, property developers, public relations experts, civil engineers, political consultants, and even movie stars and other entertainers. "Among the wealthiest symbolic analysts," says Reich, "are Steven Spielberg, Bill Cosby, Charles Schulz, Eddie Murphy, Sylvester Stallone, Madonna, and other star directors and performers. . . . [And] behind each of these familiar faces is a collection of American problem-solvers, -identifiers, and brokers who train, coach, advise, promote, amplify, direct, groom, represent, and otherwise add value to their talents" (ibid., 220-21). These symbolic-analysts may be employees, but their expertise is in such high demand that they enjoy an independence and exert a level of control over their careers and incomes undreamed of by either in-person servers or routine production workers.

Perhaps the most important factor influencing the workforce equation, however, is that there is not unlimited demand for symbolic-analysts. One hundred percent of the employable population cannot find work in these jobs. Only a minority can fit into this one rising boat. The rest of us must compete for jobs in either a dwindling manufacturing sector or an immense, low-paying service sector. The result is an increasingly unequal society, one that can sustain neither economic nor social health. This whole unfolding scenario leads us inevitably to a particularly uncomfortable question: *Is it perhaps time to rethink our centuries-old assumptions about the division of labor and come to terms with what those assumptions have done to our society?*

Equality
The underlying issue here is equality, which is a concept that in both theory and practice seems to give nearly everyone dyspepsia.

If we weren't concerned about equality, we wouldn't even have an American Dream or social ideals, and we wouldn't be troubled by the increasing gap between rich and poor. We wouldn't even bother trying to justify the natural effects of capitalism. But we *are* concerned about equality. It's an integral part of the American psyche and the American Dream. According to Webster's, the American Dream is a "social ideal that stresses egalitarianism and especially material prosperity." If the two halves of this definition seem incompatible, well, they are—given our current economic assumptions. In our capitalist system, overall material prosperity comes only at the expense of equality. Can the two ideas be reconciled? We certainly must hope so, for equality is not merely an American ideal and a morally appealing principle; some approximation of it is also necessary for long-term economic health.

Thomas Jefferson declared in the Declaration of Independence that "all men are created equal," thus planting the idea, as Frost put it, "where it will trouble us a thousand years" (Frost, 1969, 57). Frost was right. Because Jefferson didn't bother to explain exactly what he meant by "equal," we have been arguing about it already for more than two hundred years.

For instance, do we mean equality of opportunity or equality of outcome? It's hard to guarantee equality of outcome without removing people's freedom entirely, for individuals possess varying levels of intelligence, talent, and motivation. Equality of opportunity is probably nearer the mark, but how do we guarantee everyone an equal opportunity? This is actually the central question of this book, and I shall attempt to answer it more fully in a later chapter, but for now let me merely suggest that neither the liberals nor the conservatives offer a viable solution.

It is also difficult to entirely separate these two types of equality. When we talk about equality of opportunity, we can't just sweep equality of outcome under the rug, because it is impossible to offer equal opportunity without requiring to some degree an equality of outcome. As the natural mechanism of unbridled capitalism creates a two-tiered society of haves and have-nots, the opportunities of some expand, while the opportunities of the rest diminish. This creates a vicious circle. Diminished opportunities translate directly into diminished outcomes, and diminished outcomes, in turn, further curtail opportunities. We must, therefore, address the complex problem of equal outcomes—not by redistributing wealth, but by ensuring that opportunity is never hoarded by some and withheld from others.

The Irrelevance of Right and Left

Neither major political orientation offers a viable solution to the growing economic inequality that prevails in modern America. The conservatives insist that the best course is just to leave the beast alone, and everyone will prosper. This strategy is arguable at best. If we leave the beast alone, the gap between rich and poor will widen at an accelerating pace, companies will continue to replace workers with technology in their drive to increase productivity, our ability to consume all that we produce will continue to shrink, disposable income will drop while consumer debt rises, and we shall not prosper. The standard of living for most Americans will slip as the middle class continues to lose weight.

The liberal response, on the other hand, attempts to alter only the *effects*, and not the functioning, of capitalism by redistributing income—in essence, to paint stripes on a baboon and then expect it to behave like a zebra. For many reasons, the welfare state has proved itself a major disappointment.

No true liberal, of course, would suggest that everyone be

made absolutely equal in economic matters. The true, rational liberal suggests only that we narrow the wide disparity between rich and poor by redistributing money, the fruit of capital owner-ship, to bring the very poor up to a certain minimum level of consumptive (though not productive) capacity.

Both conservatives and liberals tend to look at economics as a game. Conservatives insist that there must be both winners and losers. If we were to make it so nobody lost, they argue, we would also make it so nobody could win. And then the game would become pointless, like playing tennis without an oppo-nent. The liberals, of course, don't want to do away with the game—they just want to spot the weaker opponent a few points, possibly a whole set, so that the inevitable losers don't get trounced so badly. No shutouts allowed in the game of liberal economics.

The principal flaw of income redistribution programs is that they create dependency among the poor and sabotage the motivation and creativity of entrepreneurs and executives. Free handouts never motivated anyone to become a contributing member of society, and taking away the apples from a hard-working fruit farmer's tree may make him scratch his head and honestly wonder why he's in the business in the first place.

Is there an alternative, then, to the flawed liberal and con-servative economic strategies? Of course there is, and both sides would probably wax indignant over it, because it strikes at the root of the increasing inequality that both sides, in their own way, yearn to preserve. This alternative, however, is both logical and consistent with our American ideals: *Instead of fixing the score by redistributing income, the fruit of capitalism, we should instead consider leveling the playing field by redistributing capital, the source of income and the only factor that inspires motivation and creates genuine opportunity.*

Finding a Balance

Adam Smith theorized that the inherent self-interest of people would promote the interest of society and create an equalizing effect by benefitting both sides in any economic transaction. This would transpire as if an "invisible hand" were guiding their actions, causing them to "promote an end which was no part of [their] intention" (Smith, [1776] 1937, 423). The problem we discover when we try to apply this theory to transactions in our modern economic system is that Smith was talking about a far different society than the one we live in. In Smith's day, capital ownership was far more limited and widespread. Today, the gargantuan businesses and bureaucracies of modern capitalism have dramatically shifted the balance of power in society, effectively paralyzing Smith's invisible hand and negating any widespread societal benefit that might accrue through the economic interaction of two self-interested parties.

There is no mutual benefit, for instance, and society as a whole is worse off, when an impersonal organization has so much power that it can use, abuse, fire, or require a dehumanizing conformity from individual employees, whose only real recourse is to quit. In theory, Smith's invisible hand operated between two parties, neither of which was significantly more powerful than the other. In this circumstance, a balance would arise in terms of benefit, not just power. Equality of opportunity *and* of outcome would be served. We can realize such equality, of course, only when ownership is both widespread and limited. Democracy and equality are all about ownership. You can't really have either without it.

Achieving true democracy and functional equality is virtually impossible where opportunities are divided, as Peter Block points out, between a class of executives who are paid as much as possible and a lower class of laborers who are paid as little as possible. This double-standard pay system creates a situation in which workers are, by definition, part of the problem, and not a group that stands to benefit from any of top management's solutions. Workers are seen as a cost, something that eats away at profit and must be minimized as much as possible.

This schizophrenic wage system illustrates perfectly the gulf in our society between capitalists and noncapitalists. Capitalists, we might well say, are those who are made *independent* because the system conspires to pay them as much as possible. They can accumulate capital, lend or invest money, and earn interest. Noncapitalists, then, are those who are made *dependent* by a system that is designed to pay them as little as possible. They accumulate debt, pay interest, and never really own their time, productive energy, or technical skills. For them, the invisible hand is not only invisible, it is nonexistent. No true mutual benefit ensues, because they cannot exchange anything meaningful from a position of equal strength.

The Organizational Society

Widespread and limited ownership of capital is a foreign idea in our modern-day capitalist society. We live in an organizational world, one in which capital is controlled by a few hands and large, impersonal organizations dictate not only the work-lives of millions of Americans, but also our lives away from work: everything from our entertainment to the consumer-based identities we buy off the shelf come from large organizations.

Immense organizations and the rules that govern their ownership and management prevent any true democracy or equality from existing in modern America. These gargantuan businesses and bureaucracies have dramatically shifted the balance of power in our nation, creating a divisive society of haves and have-nots. We have come a long way from the original blueprint.

The historian Paul Johnson points out that the Declaration of Independence "laid down what no other political document in the whole of history had yet claimed, that men were 'endowed by their Creator' with the right not only to 'Life' and 'Liberty' but *the pursuit of Happiness*. By this last, what the Founding Fathers had in mind was the acquisition of property, which they saw as the precondition of human felicity. Without widely dispersed property, true individual independence, and so a sound Republic, was impossible" (Johnson, 1992, 183).

This perception that small but universal ownership is necessary in a truly free society soon withered, however, before the rising sun of capitalist conquest, and the focus of those interested in improving the total human picture shifted from equal ownership, which was given up as a practical impossibility, to a vain (and still ongoing) attempt to create a viable substitute for true equality—in short, a counterfeit.

Huge corporations, says Christopher Lasch, as well as the wage system and a more and more intricate subdivision of labor, made it pointless to restore the independence of individual proprietorship. Instead of giving the wage earner a piece of the action (a piece of the capital), "enlightened social policy" would make his job secure, his working conditions tolerable, and his wages equitable. "Hardly anyone asked any more whether freedom was consistent with hired labor. People groped instead, in effect, for a moral and social equivalent of the widespread property ownership once considered indispensable to the success of democracy." But redistributing income, guaranteeing job security, and turning the working classes into consumers are nothing more than pale substitutes for property ownership; for none of these strategies produce "the kind of active, enterprising citizenry envisioned by nineteenth-century democrats" (Lasch, 1991, 207-8, 224-25).

An "active, enterprising citizenry" is only possible when the citizens own substantial quantities of capital—so that they can be producers. By contrast, a society weighted down by an immense host of practical noncapitalists must be, by definition, a society of subordinate role-players and consumers.

If we do not fully own our time, energy, skills, and, most of all, our production, how can we possibly achieve the American Dream? The ideals that make up that Dream—equality, liberty, democracy, unity, human dignity, justice, even material prosperity—are not fully available to us if we do not own the fundamental building blocks of our lives. The American Dream, as discussed earlier, is not simply an economic wish. It is a much grander ideal that encompasses every aspect of life. And if we are not completely free during a third of our waking hours, then even our lives away from work lose some of their meaning.

What we have not learned in all these years is that you can't disconnect a person's political, social, and economic circumstances without damaging all three. A society filled with authoritarian businesses restricts in a very real way a person's political influence and social development. Hired laborers, regardless how well compensated they are, will never achieve the levels of independence, community spirit, and equality necessary to make democracy work—either in the nation as a whole or in the organizations where they labor.

Sure, cried the tenant men, but it's
our land. We measured it and broke it up.
We were born on it, and we got killed on it.
Even if it's no good, it's still ours. That's what
makes it ours—being born on it, working it,
dying on it. That makes ownership, not a
paper with numbers on it.

We're sorry. It's not us. It's the
monster. The bank isn't like a man.

Yes, but the bank is only made of men.

No, you're wrong there—quite wrong
there. The bank is something else than men.
It happens that every man in a bank hates
what the bank does, and yet the bank does it.
The bank is something more than men,
I tell you. It's the monster. Men made it,
but they can't control it.

—John Steinbeck,
The Grapes of Wrath

6

A Nation of Wage Earners

Ownership. The ground-level assumption of modern American capitalism is that individual ownership of capital should be unlimited. This assumption gives shape and direction to our wayward economic system and opens the door to the other faulty assumptions we've talked about. When we peel away all its window dressing, capitalism isn't really about free markets or free enterprise, as the economic elite would have us believe; it is about ownership of capital. Period. Capitalism, like communism, is a philosophy about ownership. Over the years *capitalism* has come to mean "unrestricted private ownership of capital," a condition that is decidedly incongruent with our political precepts and our social ideals. This, however, was not always the case.

A Misconception
The great misconception about modern capitalism is that it is a democratic economic system. We've always equated communism

with authoritarianism and capitalism with democracy. The logic goes something like this: since democracy is the opposite of authoritarianism, since capitalism is the opposite of communism, and since authoritarianism and communism always seem to go together, then democracy and capitalism must be one package—you can't have one without the other. This is nonsense. It is theoretically possible to have political democracy without capitalism. It is also possible to have capitalism without political democracy. Any dictator who allows his subjects to own property and accumulate capital has created capitalistic authoritarianism.

Most capitalists would be shocked, however, to learn that modern capitalism is, in practice, as incompatible with democracy as is the enforced cooperation of communism. Capitalism, technically, is the unlimited private ownership of property *and the means of production.* The italics here are important, because they point to two conditions that conflict with democracy, create increasing inequality, and spawn a host of problems in society. The fact that I can own a piece of property, build a house on it, and reside there is of little consequence. But the unlimited ownership of capital, the means of production, is exactly what places capitalism at odds with our political and social ideals.

In an unlimited capitalist system such as ours, ownership of capital, although it can take any form, tends to be either concentrated in the hands of one or more active individual owners or dispersed among a large, shifting, external body of passive owners. These two types of ownership are very dissimilar, even opposite, in *form*, but in *effect* they are actually quite similar.

Concentrated Ownership

Concentrated ownership, the more traditional form, produces people we generally think of as capitalists: individuals who have accumulated or inherited such large amounts of capital that they can hire others (buy their time and energy, a portion of their lives) to produce products for them. The employees are paid a nominal amount that we call a "fair wage," the products are sold, profits are reaped, and the owner then uses these funds to increase his capital—so that he can purchase the time of more individuals and further increase his wealth, his capital, and his distance from those whose lives he more or less owns.

And he does own them in more than a metaphorical sense, because he owns the produce of their hands and minds, a literal part of them. And they can't escape his employ (except to flee to someone else's), because they don't have capital. They're not paid enough by the capitalist to become independent, as he is. He doesn't share his capital with them. Instead they're paid just enough to stay one step ahead of the bills (if they happen to be prudent money managers), and for this they should be grateful, or so they are indoctrinated.

Now, you may argue that this is a gloomy, Marxist view of our relatively prosperous economic conditions, especially considering the perceived outcome of the Cold War, but let's take a closer look at democracy. One would have to be hallucinating to suggest that capitalist businesses of any size are democratic institutions, even those that seriously are trying to "democratize" the workplace. Do the people hired by an industrialist or small business owner have an independent voice in the fundamental decisions or direction of the business? Are they equal with the owner in either pay or power? Of course not.

"But," some may protest, "many employers are benevolent and treat their employees well." Certainly, and there have also been many benevolent monarchs throughout history, but their subjects didn't enjoy democracy, government by the people. The employees of an industrialist don't govern the organization. Even when they are *empowered*, they still live in an authoritarian system. There is a world of difference between employee empowerment and employee ownership. You don't have to "empower" owners. The key here is that someone else is *able to* exercise arbitrary power in the employees' lives, even if that person elects not to. It is the ability, the possibility, that is relevant here. The owner, if he chooses, can even require them, if they want to keep their jobs, to conform to trivial or demeaning rules and customs.

A benevolent business owner can easily become a tyrant if the company experiences a few setbacks. WordPerfect Corporation, mentioned in an earlier chapter, was a very good company to work for, or so many of my neighbors have informed me. Employee salaries were above industry average, the atmosphere was relaxed, and year-end bonuses were consistent and generous. Then the atmosphere in the software market, dominated by Microsoft, grew ominous. WordPerfect owners announced that they would terminate 21 percent of the workforce. They deemed this necessary, but that is irrelevant to this discussion. The point here is this: Did these terminated workers have any recourse, any real power? No. They discovered the hard way that they didn't belong to an organizational democracy. They couldn't maintain their corporate citizenship by virtue of the fact that it was *their* business. They couldn't vote the owners out of office. All they could do was pack their things and hit the pavement. One day they were under the illusion that they were valuable and happy citizens of a wonderful corporate kingdom; the next day they were gone, with a new understanding of why *corporate citizen* is an oxymoron. Republics have citizens; authoritarian systems have subjects.

Employees in most businesses are trapped. Because they don't own capital, they can't just walk away and declare their independence. They have to make a living in some way, unless they prefer to either starve or live off government handouts. Independence and equality have been withheld from them by a system—capitalism—that is overtly authoritarian in nature. And even when it wears a benevolent mask, it is still *structurally* authoritarian and retains its oppressive potential.

The question today's progressive business leaders and consultants are asking is: How do we make authoritarianism palatable? Or worse: How do we disguise authoritarianism to make it seem more democratic. These questions will never yield a satisfactory answer.

We extol the virtues of the free-market system, because it is largely (as its name suggests) free; at the macro level, it is consistent with our democratic ideals. But that system ends at the front door to most businesses. The free market exists *between* businesses, but not *within* them. Companies in the market are free, but employees within those businesses are not. Gifford and Elizabeth Pinchot have coined the term *free intraprise* to describe a free-market system that ought to exist within organizations. "The alternative to corporate bureaucracy is not merely training managers to behave in an empowering way within a bureaucratic structure; it is developing a system of freedoms and institutions analogous to free enterprise" (Pinchot, 1993, 114). It is my contention, however, that *free intraprise* cannot truly exist unless ownership patterns change within organizations. Ownership is the *entire* question where liberty and democracy are concerned.

Dispersed Ownership

As indicated above, our authoritarian system of ownership also has another face. Dispersed ownership, the opposite of concentrated ownership, results in an even more insidious state of affairs. Here we're talking about the massive corporations that dominate the economic (and physical) landscape of twentieth-century America. These conglomerates are owned (sometimes indirectly through mutual funds and pension plans) by a mass of faceless names that usually play no role within the business as employees or managers and may even have no direct contact with the business as either suppliers or customers. They are strewn from one end of the country to the other, almost as if a big wind had swept them up like autumn leaves and scattered them across the countryside. Some have called them absentee owners. Normally we call them stockholders.

Since these absentee owners are little concerned with the day-to-day operations of the business—taking specific interest only in stock prices, dividends, and earnings per share—they hire professional executives to run the show. And since professional executives actually have more power than the dispersed body of owners, they represent the corporate equivalent of the individual capitalist, the industrialist. They perform the same function, enriching themselves on the labors of others, paying themselves exorbitant wages, acting as rulers and decision makers for the masses of employees whose workaday lives they have purchased (albeit with someone else's money).

But there are significant differences between an individual capitalist or industrialist and a professional executive. The industrialist invariably has a knowledge of both the product itself and the process by which it is created; he (or sometimes she) is more community oriented, more aware of the lives of his employees, often seeing himself as some kind of benevolent, provident feudal lord; and he is the legal owner of the business.

Most professional managers, on the other hand, are generalists, often having no specific knowledge of the products and processes they are hired to manage. Instead, they've been trained in modern business schools; they have white collars and are dressed for success. They know finance rather than the nuts and bolts of a particular industry; and their financial training, they firmly believe, qualifies them to work in any business with any product—because they don't really deal with products, only with the numbers that surround them.

So they play with ratios and financial statements, dream up marketing strategies, and acquire other companies and products that they don't begin to understand, secure in the knowledge that their jobs are safe as long as the bottom line, market share, and dividends are on the increase. This is why a company like General Electric, with its relentlessly return-crazy chairman, "Neutron Jack" Welch, now sells bonds, makes jet engines and locomotives, hawks a direct-broadcast satellite service, markets industrial diamonds, and runs a TV network.

Because professional executives see themselves as exactly that—professionals, hired specifically to make tough and per-haps unpopular decisions—they add up the numbers, and if the numbers tell them to lay off thousands of workers, that's exactly what they do. Neutron Jack, for instance, has at this writing erased 170,000 jobs at GE, sometimes going so far as to send lower-level managers packing on the spot and then shipping their personal effects home by UPS (Hawken, 1993, 124). This from the man who once said, "Any company that's going to make it in the 1990s and beyond has got to find a way to engage the mind of every single employee. . . . What's the alternative? Wasted minds? Uninvolved people? A labor force that's angry or bored? That doesn't make sense!" (Tichy and Sherman, 1993, 251) Neither does amputating 170,000 people from the body of those supposedly valuable employees.

For fundamental reasons, professional executives have little *personal* interest in the impact their decisions and policies—from plant closings to pollution—have on communities. They

generally don't live in the communities affected by their decisions. And because they don't actually own the business, they're
free to look out for themselves, preferring loyalty to career over
loyalty to employees or even the organization, usually leaving
themselves an open door and a golden parachute, just in case
the organizational plane takes a nose dive or the pilot's seat in a
larger aircraft becomes available.

So which masters do you prefer, industrialists or CEOs? As
for me, I prefer freedom, for either form of capitalism is at odds
with democracy and human dignity. Should this statement sur-
prise us? Of course it should. We've always been taught that
capitalism is morally superior to communism. In reality, these
competing systems are more similar than they are different.
They are two sides of the same rusty coin—both outdated, both
authoritarian in practice, although, ironically, it is communism,
not capitalism, that claims to be democratic in theory.

Times Have Changed
The rise of capitalism actually brought favorable changes in its
early years—greater freedom, equality, and democracy—but
with no inherent restriction on ownership, capitalism was
doomed to its present course. In hindsight, it is perfectly logical
that communism should have arisen in reaction to the injustices
and abuses that resulted from unlimited capital ownership. It's
interesting to note in this context that Karl Marx's monumental
work, which laid the theoretical foundation for the communist
revolution, was titled *Das Kapital*. Capital ownership was always
the central issue. The communist mistake, however, was to
swing the pendulum too far—from unrestricted private ownership of capital to no private ownership at all—and then to
enforce this arrangement with authoritarian government.

Capitalism, originally, was a *liberal* economic doctrine, a rebellion against the monarchic and aristocratic systems of Europe. In those days, capitalism was seen as a great tool in dispersing property, wealth, and power among a much broader group of citizens. But capitalism soon developed its own authoritarian and aristocratic classes, and power, wealth, and property soon became restricted and concentrated, just as they had been under the old monarchies.

"Right-wing economics," according to Christopher Lasch, "conceives of the capitalist economy as it was in the time of Adam Smith, when property was still distributed fairly widely, businesses were individually owned, and commodities still retained something of the character of useful objects" (Lasch, 1991, 519). But much has changed since then. The rise of large, impersonal economic bureaucracies, the increasing inconsequence of owning private property, and the shift from a production ethic to a consumption ethic have transformed capitalism into something far different from what it might have become.

The most notable manifestation of this transformation appears perhaps in the life of the common man or woman. As the captains of industry consolidated their power, and as their organizations increasingly became employers of the masses, people felt great pressure to change, to trade independence for supposed security and marginal prosperity, to fit the functional corporate mold, and, consequently, they became systematically dehumanized. "The division of labor, John Ruskin argued, was misnamed. It was not the labor that was divided but the men, who were 'divided into mere segments of men—broken into small fragments and crumbs of life.' . . . Men were now condemned to forms of labor that made them 'less than men' in their own eyes. 'It is not that men are ill fed, but that they have no pleasure in the work by which they make their bread, and therefore look to wealth as the only means of pleasure'" (Lasch,

1991, 137). This happens when people do not own the produce of their hands and minds. They become something less than human, and the market mechanism is crippled.

Adam Smith's "invisible hand" cannot function properly in either the unbalanced power structure of corporate America or our undisciplined "shop till you drop" marketplace; it works best in an ambience of widespread and limited (relatively equal) property ownership. Well into the next century after Smith's death, it was generally agreed that freedom could not thrive in a nation of hirelings.

The Individual Versus the Human Resource

The fundamental question we must resolve when contemplating the individual's place in organizational America is, once again: "Which is more important, the individual or the organization where he or she works?" Do individuals serve the organization or does the organization serve the community of individuals? In spite of our traditional American ideals, the sorry answer is that in twentieth-century America, individuals are less important than and serve the organizations to which they belong.

Human beings are viewed, even in these days of enlightened organizational thinking, as property. *Human resources.* Resources are things we buy and then use to make a profit. *Our employees are our most valuable asset.* An asset is a piece of property, something you own and use until it is either depleted or obsolete.

This sort of talk is intended as a compliment, and, as such, it sheds light on the status of workers in today's economy. I hear from all quarters the apparently sincere belief that the only way American companies can be competitive in the current global marketplace is to train the American workforce to be more productive. "We must invest more in our workers," I hear. "We must give them the mathematical and statistical and scientific training that will make them more useful to corporate America."

This generous offer to educate and train workers is admirable, but it is also misdirected—because it is motivated solely by the organizational imperative of survival. It has virtually nothing to do with the needs and desires and talents and values of individuals.

Our society is so bottom-line oriented that we feel we cannot afford to cater to the whims and preferences of individuals. Organizations must thrive, therefore we must learn to view individuals as resources and assets, things to be used, and not to be improved for their own sake. It doesn't matter what innate talents or proclivities they might have, they must sacrifice their dreams on the altar of corporate profitability and become what corporate America wants them to become. And because of the faulty assumptions that drive our economic institutions, we have created an increasingly high-tech, fast-paced world in which only one kind of intelligence—quantitative—is rewarded, almost to the exclusion of all others. Consequently, everyone must excel in that area, or the organizers of economic enterprise regard (and discard) them as useless.

Many, perhaps even most, Americans are being crammed into jobs that do not fit them very well. Not everyone is in the 90th percentile of mathematical aptitude. Most of us, truth be known, are not very good at numbers. We would rather be doing something more meaningful (which usually means something in which we have some innate talent, where we feel we can offer something to society). But in our increasingly high-tech world, we focus more and more narrowly on that one particular type of intelligence. Those of us who are intelligent and talented in unmarketable areas may find ourselves unemployable, or at least grossly underpaid.

Human beings, in other words, must subordinate their own talents and desires, not to the good of society, but to the welfare of organizations that have an intense need for nothing other than survival. Organizational exigencies determine what areas I can pursue as a career, as my life's work. This is the common lot of a "human resource" in organizational America. But simply giving everybody rigorous math, science, and technical skills is as unindividualistic as making everyone a good communist. People should be free to choose how they will make a contribution to society. So, instead of running hell-bent after every new technological wonder, just so the economy can be more productive and competitive, a society that ranks human beings above organizations, I argue, would look at the diverse nature of individuals and make room for all, so that they can contribute in ways they are best suited for.

To try to make everyone adept at high-tech, mathematical work is to pursue the fallacious theory that human beings are perfectly malleable and have no innate talents and tendencies and can consequently be shaped to fit the organization's (or nation's) needs. Perhaps we need to mold organizations instead to fit individual needs. Is this possible? What might happen if we expended our money and energy in helping individuals discover and develop the areas where they are truly gifted and assisted them in finding useful outlets for the expression of those talents?

Work Versus Labor

David K. Hart points out a subtle distinction between work and labor. Labor, he says, is what all animals do, what human beings must do, to eat and survive. Labor is drudgery. There is nothing ennobling about it. Work, on the other hand, is the opportunity for individuals to place their unique stamp upon whatever it is they are producing—whether it be an oak table, a book, a car, a haircut, or a music lesson. Work not only shapes the produce of an individual's time and energy, it shapes the individual.

We define ourselves partially by the work we do. And if we must labor instead of work, we are less than human. This, I submit, is the greatest abuse perpetrated on individuals by modern organizations: that they deny them the opportunity to work. They require individuals instead to fit themselves into some preconceived pattern; to think and behave in certain approved ways; to be a function; to give up the things they are passionate about and adopt stale organizational goals and mission statements and pretend to be excited about them; to produce to someone else's specifications products they care not one iota about; to trade their time, their lives, and large portions of their souls for sterile security and the hollow promise of marginal prosperity.

And we wonder why people feel powerless, why there is a growing sense of despair, or worse, indifference, regarding our future. Most of our population has been turned into a huge, collective "human resource," and yet we wonder why they are not happy and optimistic and motivated. How long can we expect people to be satisfied with fading security and dwindling prosperity while offering more and more of themselves on the altar of organizational dependence? How long can we expect people to shelve their innate talents and deny their rightful desires to be fully human?

Democracy, Power, and Ownership

Corporate America has finally come to realize on a subconscious level that it has deprived its employees of certain basic or integral ingredients. Intense global competition has revealed that something is missing from the modern capitalist recipe for success. Consequently, three popular buzzwords are making the rounds in corporate America: *empowerment, democracy,* and *a sense of ownership.* But these terms are deceptive. Most of what passes itself off as democracy in organizational America is actually only a token sharing of responsibility. It's a half-baked, watered-down version of self-rule. Likewise, empowerment in corporate America, of necessity, involves the bestowal of a tractable, emasculated form of power. And the "sense of ownership" that management talks about is simple make-believe.

Democracy implies equality, the shared power to combine with your equals in making decisions, in governing the group to which you belong. But democracy of this sort exists only where ownership is divided equally among those who spend the days of their lives serving together in the organization. Such equality is also the source of appropriate, accountable power. If there is always someone, or a group of someones, whose actual, legal ownership gives them more power than the employees, then they can make *arbitrary* decisions without being *accountable* to the body of individuals who work for the organization. In such companies there is no real democracy, no true empowerment, and the political structure of the organization is by definition authoritarian in nature.

In the current "cutting-edge" management literature, I read repeatedly that management is supposed to give employees a "sense of ownership," or, stranger yet, that employees are supposed to take upon themselves this "sense of ownership." The reason, of course, is that organizations cannot survive in today's ultracompetitive marketplace without dedicated, intelligent, motivated workers. This "sense of ownership" is supposed to give employees the commitment they need to be truly valuable to the organization. But what on earth is a "sense of ownership"? It is, in truth, a pretense, an illusion. It is management asking workers to pretend they own something they don't actually own. It is the illusion of ownership, a bald-faced attempt to conceal the true nature of business relationships, to make workers think that the authoritarian structure of capitalist business does not really exist.

But ownership is ownership. A "sense of ownership" is a lie we tell one another and ourselves to make us feel better about the inherent injustice and inconsistency of our organizational relationships. If management wants workers to have genuine commitment, then it must give them actual ownership, the only real source of commitment. And the consultants who roam the hills and valleys of organizational America telling workers that they must take upon themselves "ownership" of the business are selling a bill of goods. You can't simply "take" ownership, not unless the current owners give you a piece of it.

And the reason all this talk of "empowerment" and "sense of ownership" is empty rhetoric is that those who sit in power and who possess today's corporate kingdoms are not simply going to give up their power and ownership out of the generosity of their hearts. Peter Block tells a story that pretty much sums up the sham of corporate "empowerment" programs.

> A friend of mine who works for a big telecommunications company was asked to devise ways for people at the bottom of the organization to take more ownership for the success of the business. One of his recommendations was to eliminate reserved parking for the top executives . . . a symbolic gesture to communicate we are all part of the same team working toward the same goal. He suggested this to Bob, the general manager, and Bob's response was, "If you ask for my parking space now, you will want my salary later. I don't want to give you my salary, I know you don't want to give your people your salary. The answer is no." (Block, 1993, 38-39)

Bob was at least honest. Most executives and owners are

not. They are using the same manipulative marketing tactics we see in the consumer arena to sell their employees on the idea that they can have ownership without really owning anything and without sharing equally in the profits created by their increased dedication. They are merely constructing another elaborate illusion to milk their employees of whatever it takes to keep the business in business. And please note that they are not asking employees to develop and apply their intelligence, ingenuity, and good judgment because it is important for individuals to cultivate and use such qualities in their lives. They solicit increased dedication for the express reason that the organization simply cannot succeed without intelligent, versatile, creative, motivated workers. It is the organization's welfare, not the employees', that matters.

The Avalanche

Now that I've stated my position on token democracy, empty empowerment, and imaginary ownership, let me turn this same argument on its head for a moment and suggest that some good might actually come from the empowerment movement, misdirected though it is. It is quite possible that the proponents of this movement have unleashed a force more powerful than they understand. It is possible that they have started an avalanche that will not stop halfway up the slope where all the empowerment gurus and progressive managers believe it will.

If you understand their argument, what these theorists are saying, without actually saying it, is that the movement underway today to empower employees and democratize the workplace will eventually lead to actual employee power, real democracy, and genuine ownership. This is the logical conclusion to their arguments, even if they haven't yet arrived at that conclusion. They are talking about a revolution, if you listen carefully to their rhetoric. The forces that have been unleashed in organizational America, they claim, are inexorable and will change the face of business from one end of this country to the other. If this is true—and we have no reason to doubt that it is—then these relentless forces will not stop at token empowerment and democracy in name only. The avalanche won't stop midslope. It may, however, run into some determined and resourceful opposition.

The increase in token democracy, the push for employee empowerment, and the creation of a "sense of ownership" are certainly steps in the right direction, and it may be glibly argued that they are merely waystations along the inevitable path to true democracy, real ownership, and full employee power-holding, but try fitting that theoretical shoe on the foot of any capitalist or million-dollar-salaried CEO. They may agree to cosmetic empowerment and the illusion of democracy that is currently in vogue, they may even give up their parking spaces, but see what happens when you ask for their salaries, their offices, their bloated staffs, their golden parachutes, their mansions, their separatism, and their prestige. And don't deceive yourself into thinking those things won't be asked for. They lie on the lower slopes, below where the consultants and progressive leaders think the avalanche will stop. But it will not stop until it reaches level ground.

Who will win? No one can say. Someday the capitalists and popular consultants may wake up to discover that they have been playing with fire, that this token democracy and the illusions of empowerment and the "sense of ownership" they've supported have put ideas into people's heads, correct ideas. And they may get burned. People in general are a lot smarter than they are given credit for. Someday it will dawn on them that if token democracy is good, then real democracy must be better. If watered-down empowerment is their right, as they have been told, then why not real power? And if their organizations can't succeed unless they develop a "sense of ownership," then certainly real employee ownership should be even better for their organizations. They will eventually realize that someone has been stealing their lives, and they will demand what is rightly theirs.

Who Really Creates Capital?

In the next chapter, we'll look in greater detail at what I've already suggested briefly—that we must consider redistributing capital rather than income. The capitalists, who now claim ownership, will undoubtedly cry foul. "That would be stealing," they will certainly say. I would respond, however, by asking, "Are the police stealing when they take back your car from the person who stole it from you?" It is only stealing when you take something that doesn't belong to you. To take back what is rightly yours can hardly be called stealing.

The real question regarding ownership is the one asked by John Steinbeck in this chapter's epigraph. What constitutes ownership, especially of capital? Shouldn't ownership be related somehow to the question of who creates it, who works and slaves and toils to bring it into existence? Is it the person who plants the seeds or the person who works the land and pulls the weeds and nurtures, fertilizes, and irrigates the soil who should reap the harvest? The answer, I submit, is that both deserve a share.

The capitalist invests a sum of money, but that money will not create a product and generate a profit without the time and energy of other human beings. Don't they have just as great a role in the creation of new capital as the one who invested the money to start the venture? And if they aren't given a fair share of the capital, hasn't someone been stealing from them? Says Michael Ventura:

> As a worker, I am not an "operating cost." I am how the job gets done. I *am* the job. I am the company. . . . I'm willing to take my lumps in a world in which little is certain, but I deserve a say. Not just some cosmetic "input," but significant power in good times or bad. A place at the table where the decisions are made. Nothing less is fair. So nothing less is moral. . . . It takes more than investment and management to make a company live. It takes the labor, skill, and talent of the people who do the company's work. Isn't *that* an investment? Doesn't it deserve a fair return, a voice, a share of the power? . . . If the people who do the work don't own some part of the product, and don't have any power over what happens to *their* enterprise—they are being robbed. *You* are being robbed. And don't think for a minute that those who are robbing you don't know they are robbing you. They know how much they get from you and how little they give back. They are thieves. They are stealing your life." (Ventura, 1991, 78, 80)

Indeed, they pay themselves as much as possible and pay you as little as possible. By contrast, an equitable redistribution of capital would eliminate this double-standard pay system. It would also abolish authoritarian economic organizations, foster true democracy, and bring our out-of-control economy back into harmony with our political aspirations and social ideals. As I hope I've made clear in the preceding chapters, this is not merely something we should consider because it is the moral thing to do—and it *is* the moral thing to do—we should move rapidly in this direction because it is also perhaps our best hope for averting economic ruin.

Part 2

Replacing the System

To speak of certain government and establishment institutions as "the system" is to speak correctly, since these organizations are founded upon the same structural conceptual relationships as a motorcycle. They are sustained by structural relationships even when they have lost all other meaning and purpose. People arrive at a factory and perform a totally meaningless task from eight to five without question because the structure demands that it be that way. There's no villain, no "mean guy" who wants them to live meaningless lives, it's just that the structure, the system demands it and no one is willing to take on the formidable task of changing the structure just because it is meaningless.

But to tear down a factory or revolt against a government or to avoid repair of a motorcycle because it is a system is to attack effects rather than causes; and as long as the attack is upon effects only, no change is possible. The true system, the real system, is our present construction of systematic thought itself, rationality itself, and if a factory is torn down but the rationality which produced it is left standing, then that rationality will simply produce another factory. If a revolution destroys a systematic government, but the systematic patterns of thought that produced that government are left intact, then those patterns will repeat themselves in the succeeding government. There's so much talk about the system. And so little understanding.

—Robert M. Pirsig,
*Zen and the Art of
Motorcycle Maintenance*

*Employees are being paid to produce,
not to make themselves into better people.
Corporations are purchasing employee
time to make a return on it, not investing in
employees to enrich their lives. Employees
are human capital, and when capital is hired
or leased the objective is not to embellish it
for its own sake but to use it for financial
advantage. But somewhere in this philosophy
there is an inconsistency with the notion of
a society of self-governing individuals. The
large corporation has become an organizer
of people, a user of people, a molder of
identities, according to criteria that it has
evolved, without regard to the effect on
those people except as this is registered
on the balance sheet.*

—Neil W. Chamberlain,
*The Limits of
Corporate Responsibility*

7

A Nation of Owners

The first step we must take, if we wish to design an economic system independent of growth and progress and more tuned to serving the real needs of society, is to reconsider the most fundamental principle of capitalism—namely, the license to accumulate unlimited capital. *Limitless ownership.* This is the grand key that turns the lock on Pandora's box and unleashes the demons of relentless, interminable growth in our economy. Consequently, a change in our ability to own things is the most fundamental change we must make, a change that will affect us not only economically, but socially and politically also, for it will serve as a first and pivotal step in bringing the ideals that comprise the American Dream back into harmony.

As mentioned earlier, a fundamental philosophical incongruity separates the founding principles of our nation from the economic tenets that govern modern capitalism. This disparity would be of little consequence if its impact were limited to the esoteric arguments of scholars. Unfortunately, this is not the case. The incompatibility between our political ideals and our economic realities affects each individual in society at a very personal level. Indeed, the authoritarian nature of our economic institutions effectively prevents most American citizens from achieving their innate potential as they seek a fulfilling *life*, an equal share of *liberty* within the bounds of democracy, and a true and independent sense of *happiness*.

Some may choose to discount this argument, insisting that most workers prefer to be employed from eight to five each day by someone else and are fully satisfied with their work. This argument, however, runs counter to both common sense about human nature and the cold, hard facts. A recent Roper poll, for instance, found that only 18 percent of American workers consider their careers personally and financially rewarding (Leckey, 1993, 6). Eighteen percent. Apparently, spending forty hours or more each week performing tasks that someone else tells them to perform is not so enjoyable to most Americans—especially when they are paid the bare minimum while those who own their time live in comparative opulence. If the rebellion in the former Soviet Bloc should have taught us anything, it is that people do not enjoy being subject to unaccountable power.

Building a House of Happiness

One idea we often overlook in both politics and economics is the notion that our nation's founding was the *beginning* of a process, not the end. It was the planting of a seed, not the harvesting of ripened fruit. The Founders changed many things, but they did not change everything. Indeed, what they changed more than anything was direction. There was not total agreement among the Founders on all issues and, in some ways, more than moving toward a specific goal, they were moving away from certain evils, establishing a system that would prevent them from cropping up again. Unfortunately, they had no way of predicting some evils, such as the concentration of power in large economic institutions (that in many ways resemble the vessels of arbitrary power they so vehemently opposed). Had they foreseen our day, they likely would have included in the Constitution specific limitations to the accumulation of economic and not just political power.

Perhaps the Founders didn't totally understand the forces of societal change their Revolution had set in motion, but they did understand one thing. They knew that the new nation would reach its ultimate destination not in one giant leap, but in countless stages over time. The Founders were bound by the reality that some things must change gradually, that some ideals are beyond our present reach. This does not mean, however, that those ideals are not worthy, or that we shouldn't strive toward them.

The Founders, if you will, drew up the blueprint and laid the foundation. Later generations would then follow that blueprint and build on that foundation, perhaps changing a few features as circumstances warranted (this is why they provided a means for amending the Constitution). Whether they actually got so specific as to designate what sort of roof or veneer the structure would eventually have is both debatable and irrelevant. They knew what kind of edifice they wanted: a free one to which each citizen would have equal access and in which every American could reach his or her human potential. Some of the details, they knew, an informed and moral citizenry would have to put in place.

Unfortunately, in some ways we are not changing in the right direction. We have tossed the Founders' blueprint aside and are building a sprawling prison on the foundation that was to have supported a beautiful mansion. In our economic institutions we have not followed the blueprint, which included such values and principles as democracy, equality, the sanctity of each human life, individual liberty, and the pursuit of happiness. Instead, we have built up authoritarian economic institutions that operate in direct conflict with the values and principles of our founding. The industrialists and the professional executive class would have us believe that those values and principles do not apply to economic matters, or that we should apply them only in a token or metaphorical sense, but that is nonsense.

"As free agents," David K. Hart maintains, "individuals can magnify or squander the possibilities of their lives, but those lives are sacred. Therefore, no organization, public or private, has any right to deny, or even trivialize, the possibilities of individual lives with organizational requirements" (Hart, 1988a, 5). We must remember that the American Revolution was fought to protect individuals from the exercise of unaccountable power in their lives. If authoritarian institutions—be they political, social, or economic—oppress us, we can never achieve true democracy, equality, freedom, or happiness.

As suggested in an earlier chapter, our current belief in the idea of progress, in unbridled technological advance and economic growth, has no overriding purpose, no end objective, no destination. But our society, as defined by the founding values, does have an overarching purpose: to empower each individual to achieve true happiness. We are to arrive somewhere as American citizens, and that destination is a happy and healthy society.

"Happiness [is] the aim of life," wrote Jefferson. "The happiness of society is the end of government," John Adams concurred. And the pursuit of happiness, which Jefferson categorized as an unalienable right, just happens to be inseparably connected to the right to hold property. As noted in Chapter 5, the historian Paul Johnson asserts that happiness is only achievable if people, by honest effort, can acquire property. "Without widely dispersed property," he adds, "true individual independence, and so a sound Republic, [is] impossible" (Johnson, 1992, 183).

Widely dispersed property, not the concentration of property (and therefore power) that we see in modern capitalism, is the precondition to happiness and a sound Republic. If our society is to reach its true destination, if our government is to achieve its proper end, we must address this question of ownership.

Limited Ownership

A pivotal question, if we are concerned with achieving personal happiness, preserving the sanctity of each individual life, and creating a sound Republic, is the question of ownership—and not just ownership of property and capital, but the ownership of human time and energy, which has been labeled "human capital," a callous and demeaning term.

The fallacy we too often fall into is assuming that we can correct basic inequities by either transforming the American workplace or taking money from the wealthy and giving it to the poor. Corporate restructuring, flattening, or reengineering; team building; employee empowerment; and all the other buzzwords we have dreamed up to give workers the illusion of ownership (and thus motivate them) quietly bypass the real issue, as do all the liberal social redistribution programs. Not one of the currently popular approaches to achieving greater equality and democracy in the workplace addresses the fundamental obstacle to universal human happiness: lack of true ownership. We must transform our thinking on that issue.

To put it bluntly, we must prevent the three basic sources of authoritarian organizational control in our lives: unlimited capital concentration, absentee ownership, and state ownership (or state control, which is the aim of many liberal programs).

This is not a difficult problem to solve. Using a simple process of elimination, if we refuse to allow individuals to control large quantities of capital (and thus control the lives of hundreds or thousands of employees), if we disallow absentee ownership (which has created America's new ruling class, the professional executives), and if we don't permit state ownership or control of industry (a fraud perpetrated by the power hungry who insist that state ownership is really ownership by the people), then only one alternative remains: widespread, limited, direct ownership by the people, individually, not collectively.

Limited ownership is not a new idea. Thomas Paine, for instance, declared in *The Rights of Man* (1792) that "commerce is capable of taking care of itself," but he also condemned "all accumulation . . . of property, beyond what a man's own hands produce." This idea of limited, universal ownership persisted well into the nineteenth century. A mid-century labor leader named Robert MacFarlane declared that "small but universal ownership" was the "true foundation of a stable and firm republic" (Lasch, 1991, 205).

Three Levels of Ownership

Limited, universal ownership of property and the means of production is the only form of ownership that is consistent with the founding values of the American nation. Specifically, under a system of limited ownership, *an individual would be allowed to own only as much property as he or she could make productive use of.* This is the basic principle. It prevents an individual or group of individuals from accumulating more property than they themselves can effectively use, which in turn prevents them from buying time and talent and energy from the unpropertied or disfranchised (who have nothing else to sell) to work their fields or staff their offices or man their factories. It permits individuals, however, to prosper to the full extent of their intelligence, talent, diligence, and ingenuity. Above all, this principle allows every individual to own his or her personal labor and not be required to sell it. Only the fruit of that labor, which each individual owns, is for sale.

Although ownership based on ability to make productive use of the thing owned is the fundamental principle at work here, we must distinguish between different levels of use, different levels of ownership. The Indian philosopher P. R. Sarkar suggested a three-tiered economic system, an idea that makes good sense. The following description is my own extrapolation from Sarkar's basic formula.

The first level of this three-tiered economy would consist of small enterprises that produce mainly nonessential goods and services and perhaps a few essentials. These enterprises would generally have a single founder or perhaps two or three, and maybe a few "partners" who come on board somewhere downstream. To be consistent with the guiding principle of ownership limited by contribution, each new addition to the business would receive a share of ownership.

If a doctor needs to hire a receptionist or a bookkeeper to make his practice more efficient, if a restauranteur needs to enlist the help of waiters and waitresses, if a CPA requires the services of a secretary or a clerk, then the new member of the team would be given a share of ownership. Why? Because without that new member's contribution, the business would be less effective and a portion of the work wouldn't get done. But how much ownership should each new member of the business have? An equal share? Probably not. That would not be just, particularly in the case of a doctor or dentist or CPA who must invest much more time to be trained than, say, a receptionist or a bookkeeper. Ownership must also reflect seniority and other factors such as personal sacrifice, start-up funding, and risk. Perhaps my own business can serve as an illustration.

When a partner and I formed a small enterprise to design and market a humorous calendar system, we determined that we would not hire any employees, although we could very well have done that. We agreed, simply, that if we needed help, we would bring in new partners. But these new partners, although they would add value to our business, wouldn't have been there at the start. We, the two original partners, worked and scraped and worried and sacrificed and risked bankruptcy to get the company to the point where we would need more hands to do all the work. For that we felt we deserved a proportionally larger share. So we developed an ownership formula based on seniority. If you've put in ten years to make the tree grow, you should own more of the fruits than someone who has put in just two years. This formula doesn't guarantee us twice as much ownership as new partners, or even one and a half times as much, just a fraction more, based on years of association. And as more partners are added, equality increases, until, if the company ever becomes large, there will really not be much distance between the founders and new owners.

An economic system based on this philosophy does four things: *First*, it gives you incentive to find the right outlet for your talents and energy and to stay there, because if you keep jumping from company to company you never build equity in an enterprise, never own a significant portion of your work. *Second*, it prevents you from using people, from hiring them to do unpleasant tasks for you and paying them as little as possible. When you're giving a share of your company away, you don't do it with the intention of using someone to further your ends, because, *third*, it causes you carefully to select individuals of excellent character and ability who are willing, as it were, to jump in and get their hands dirty and take over responsibilities you can't handle. Consequently, *fourth*, it provides a natural disincentive for companies to grow larger than they need to. We don't want deadwood in our company. We can't afford it. We also don't want to jump into fifteen new markets with three hundred new and diverse products. We know what we do well, and learning our own well-defined market is sufficient challenge. If all companies had this philosophy, imagine the incentive it would create for children in our society, who would know that if they didn't prepare themselves well—educationally, socially, and morally—to contribute something of value, they wouldn't ever find a place to make a living.

As a precaution in our business, so that we won't bring in a new partner who is merely putting on a good show in the short term but would be a bad fit in the long run, we have adopted a mandatory one-year probation period, during which any prospective partner is guaranteed near full compensation but must prove his or her worth. If, in that time, there arise personality conflicts or indications of moral defects or a mismatch of skills, we can terminate the association. Or the prospective partner can do the same if he or she doesn't feel comfortable or happy in our company.

Under such an arrangement, your work colleagues become just like family. There's more holding you together than self-interest. You depend on one another, and you're very careful about whom you adopt. You also discover that you yourself can accomplish more actual productive work than you would if you were merely somebody else's employee (or a manager who gets paid primarily to see that others get their work done), because you own your work and the fruits of your labors. This type of organization virtually eliminates dependence and replaces it with interdependence. And it totally abolishes the tyranny that often prevails in the world of small business.

The second level of economic activity would consist of larger enterprises owned collectively by the "employees." But of course they would no longer be employees. They would now be owners. No shares of ownership would be held by "absentee owners"—outside individuals who do not give their time and talents and energy to the creation, marketing, or distribution of the company's products. This level would encompass basically the bulk of what we now call corporate America, organizations producing products whose efficient creation and distribution require the efforts of many people.

Because these are large organizations, a form of management different from that found in level-one businesses would be necessary. Whereas level-one enterprises could operate quite easily as true democracies, level-two organizations are often too large for this. Pure democracy in organizations of more than, say, fifty people would turn quickly into chaos. Rather, these organizations would have a republican form of management, patterned after our political system. Later in this chapter I'll discuss this "federal model" of management in detail; for now suffice it to say that managers would be elected by the owners.

The third level of this economic system would consist of basic industries that benefit everyone in the community: transportation, communication, education, defense, utilities, and so on. These industries, more or less, belong to everyone. They are too large to be managed effectively by cooperatives and are too important to be driven by the profit motive. Many of them must, of necessity, be monopolies. Therefore, they must fall in the public realm. Public boards or local governments would be the logical bodies to manage these entities. The people who would work in these organizations would be owners, of course, along with all other members of the community, but they would also be public servants in the truest sense of the word.

Let's now take a look at an alternative to the form of authoritarian management that at present prevails in our economic institutions, large and small. This management model, as suggested above, would apply primarily to the second tier of organizations in a new, more equal system of ownership.

The Federal Model

Each responsible citizen in the United States has a vote, but each citizen doesn't vote on every issue, every bill, every executive decision, every Supreme Court ruling. Such a voting system would create political and social gridlock. Instead, we elect representatives, then they vote for us, make executive decisions, and appoint judges and other government officials. If we don't like their voting record, we don't reelect them. It's not true democracy, but it is a workable compromise between potential anarchy and the imposed order of arbitrary authority.

We are, at least in theory, a democratic republic. And *economic democratic republics* would follow the same principles. Equal ownership, equal voice, equal representation. To prevent the abuses of power and position that we see in Congress, we would have to designate a limited term for those elected as managers within corporations and other organizations. Four or five years would be sufficient. And after a manager's administrative term was completed, he or she would then return to the regular workforce. This would eliminate the professional managerial class and would prevent the politicizing of organizational leadership, which is exactly what has happened to American government on the national level.

The advantages of this form of economic organization

would be similar to those created in government by the U.S. Constitution. These advantages were laid out by Alexander Hamilton, James Madison, and John Jay in *The Federalist Papers*, which were arguments made in support of our particular form of constitutional government. Among these advantages were the following.

Federalism

The U.S. government represents a federation of states. The states retain some power and autonomy, but are bound into a greater whole. The creation of this federation was a move toward centralization, the intent being to overcome the major weak point of the Articles of Confederation—dissension among the states. The states needed to be strong, to be unified in a larger cause, and only a strong central government could achieve those ends. This move, of course, was also based on military, security, and commercial concerns.

In most businesses today, however, the movement would have to be in the opposite direction, toward decentralization, since most organizations are authoritarian in nature and dominated by strong central control. Departments or divisions, acting much as states do in the federal government, would retain certain powers and perform certain roles. Limited, universal ownership, however, would create strong incentives toward smaller, community-oriented businesses, and away from national or international conglomerates. There would be little purpose in or justification for large, nonregional businesses under such an ownership arrangement, and great impetus to break down today's conglomerates into regional- or community-sized pieces that focused on one particular product or a set of related products. Some companies might divide up into several small, independent, department-sized groups.

Checks and Balances

Our federal government, as established in the Constitution, is a brilliant plan for preserving political freedom and democracy by preventing one individual or a segment of government from gaining too much power. Power is balanced in at least four ways: between the states and the federal government, between the two houses of Congress, among the three branches of the federal government, and between the people and their elected leaders. It is not my purpose here to explore all the ramifications of these governmental checks and balances, only to say that a similar system would need to be established in large economic institutions.

In the vast majority of today's businesses, large and small, the owner or CEO or perhaps a small group of leaders hold total power. They function more or less as dictators, exercising the legislative (policy-making), the executive (administrative), and the judicial (decision-rendering) powers in the organization. They can do just about what they want to, with no internal checks and balances, for only certain (usually inadequate) external restraints prevent them from abusing the awesome power that is theirs. Separating the executive, legislative, and judicial powers in businesses makes perfect sense. It is the best way to prevent the abuse of authority, even if that authority is granted by the employees themselves through elected management.

Popular Sovereignty

Because in the United States the people are sovereign, their will influences all branches of government. Supposedly, the only tyranny possible under such a government would be the tyranny of the majority, which worried Tocqueville.

Time, however, has proved this supposition wrong. The tyranny of the majority is not, in fact, the only tyranny possible in America. Our political system has been reshaped over time so that the wealthy and influential can exert a form of tyranny. This oppression will be with us until we accept certain types of political and economic reform. But tyranny of the majority is a very real thing in America. And, ultimately, it has but one check: the virtue of the people.

If the majority is wise and moral and virtuous in its selection of leaders, the potential tyranny of the majority will be of no consequence. The danger comes only when the majority forsakes its virtue. The Founders were well aware of this, but they had enough confidence in mankind to try this experiment anyway. Said Madison:

> I go on this great republican principle, that the people will have virtue and intelligence to select men of virtue and wisdom. Is there no virtue among us? If there be not, we are in a wretched situation. No theoretical checks, no form of government can render us secure. To suppose that any form of government will secure liberty or happiness without any virtue in the people is a chimerical idea. If there be sufficient virtue and intelligence in the community, it will be exercised in the selection of these men; so that we do not depend on their virtue, or put confidence in our rules, but in the people who are to choose them. (Hamilton, Madison, and Jay, [1787-88] 1982, xxi)

The Founders quite clearly trusted the overall virtue of the people regarding the selection of political leaders. And I believe their confidence was well placed, for even though times have changed and our choice of political leaders is regrettably limited by money and influence, we still scrutinize these candidates through the lens of a morality that no longer governs our own lives. We expect (even demand) of our elected leaders standards of morality and virtue that we do not apply even to ourselves. The day may come when the majority totally loses its sense of virtue and surrenders to outright depravity, but sufficient moral feeling has survived to prevent the tyranny Tocqueville feared.

If we organize our economic institutions according to the principles set forth in the Constitution, they would be subject to the same threat of tyranny from the majority. But this threat is insignificant next to the actual tyranny we see in our present authoritarian organizations. What this system would remove from our economic institutions is the ignorant body of employees that is willfully blind to injustice, pollution, dishonesty, and unfair business practices. No longer would there be powerless employees who say, "Hey, I didn't know. I just do my job and don't ask questions. I have no influence over what management does."

Representation

The leaders we elect after examining them under the media microscope are our *representatives* in government. They speak and act for us. The president of the United States executes the public will; the legislature enacts laws through the authority given it by the people; the Supreme Court acts for the people in determining whether laws (and decisions of lower courts) are in harmony with the guiding principles set forth in the Constitution. None of these branches of government, however, pleases everybody. Sometimes they don't please the majority. How is this possible?

Regardless of whether they were elected by popular vote or appointed by an elected official, these individuals have their own interpretations of right and wrong, good and bad, just and unjust. Representing a diverse populace is no easy matter. Sometimes special interests, because they have purchased influence (or gained it some other way), sway public representatives away from the majority position. Sometimes representatives, because of individual conscience, vote or act contrary to the will of their constituents. Sometimes there are several options, and pursuing even the most popular one still leaves 75 percent of the people dissatisfied. Representation, in short, is a compromise between the tyranny of the majority and the tyranny of individual rulers. It is the most necessary element of a republic.

In businesses this element would also be necessary in order to control the chaos into which a purely democratic workplace would inevitably fall. Every worker can't have a voice in every decision, nor would he or she want to. That would be highly inefficient. But every worker would need a voice in the overall management of the enterprise and a knowledge of what is being done and why—because the workers would be the owners. And they would exert the powers of that ownership not only in choosing those who represent them, but also in establishing limits on the power of their representatives.

These four features of our democratic republic, established by the Constitution, should apply to any organization comprising more than, say, fifty or so individuals. We must put ownership back where it belongs—in the hands of the people—but we must also avoid the chaos that a purely democratic system would spawn. The federal model is a viable solution, a perhaps imperfect although workable compromise.

Business leaders have recognized the benefits of giving employees at least the illusion of democracy, although they generally give employees only a fraction of the voice they deserve. The recent movement to permit employees to participate in ownership—from PepsiCo's "Share Power Plan" to Wendy's stock options for employees—is commendable and is gaining momentum in the United States. Much of this growth in employee ownership has come through employee stock ownership plans (ESOPs), now in place at some eleven thousand companies, involving 11.5 million employees (13 percent of the civilian workforce). Employees now own more than $120 billion in their own companies' stock, which though impressive represents only 3 percent of all shares in U.S. firms (see Rosen, 1991, 30).

These plans are popular because they (predictably) increase employee commitment and generate cash flow, but they do not go far enough. Employee shareholding at limited or token levels should not be mistaken for actual employee ownership. A business can never become an economic "democratic republic" if most of the stock is held by either a few powerful individuals or a multitude of distant, uninterested shareholders. Authoritarianism with a democratic facade should not be confused with republican democracy.

The Conversion

If we are serious about overcoming our nation's deep problems, we must make sweeping fundamental changes in our economic system, in both theory and practice, by bringing it more in line with our political philosophy and our social ideals. Says Shann Turnbull:

> To minimize corruption of all sorts, we need to decentralize power to the greatest extent possible so as to maximize checks and balances. The most fundamental sources of power in society arise from the ownership and control of land, enterprise and money. The current ownership system was developed to serve the needs of past rulers who sought absolute powers. As a result, there is no limit as to the extent and value of property which any person can possess. New rules are needed to decentralize the power of owning things—rules which follow the self-limiting and self-regulating principles found in all living things." (Turnbull, 1992, 6)

Given the fact that capitalism as we know it is both corrupt and rapidly deteriorating, we are faced with the dilemma of how to get from our present system to one that is both more equi-table and more workable. This will not be an easy transition, for it will involve the conversion of our present authoritarian organi-zations into democratic institutions. Unfortunately, recognizing that we need to make this transition is much easier than actually making it. How do you convert from a system of either narrow, unlimited ownership or widely dispersed absentee ownership to a system of limited, universal ownership?

A good argument can be built for making this transition gradually, over a long period of time. If we were to try to make this shift overnight, the consequences would likely be as horri-ble as they are predictable. Suddenly abolishing our present system of ownership would create a crisis far more perilous even than the Civil War, which arose from abolishing a different, although related, form of ownership. It would be naive to think that those who have accumulated vast amounts of money, prop-erty, and power would simply yield to reason (or even newly enacted laws) and give up these possessions without a fight. And I mean a literal fight, one in which the odds would be stacked against change and democracy. It is not difficult to imagine an actual civil war far more devastating than the one fought over slavery.

How then can we make this transition? Turnbull takes a shot at this dilemma. He proposes a system in which ownership of corporations transfers gradually, at a rate of 5 percent per year, from investors to stakeholders (employees, customers, suppli-ers). The investor would reap profits for ten years, after which this gradual transfer would begin. What this means is that thirty years after the initial capital infusion, the investor would have no ownership in the enterprise. This, says Turnbull, "would make corporate investment consistent with the time-limited rights provided to all investors in intellectual property like patents and copyright" (Turnbull, 1992, 6). Mature corporations, according to Turnbull's plan, would then finance new technology and market growth by transferring parts of their operations to spinoffs or "corporate offspring," which would attract new investors.

This system, although a far cry better than our present heap of perpetual, monopolistic shareholding, is still a system in which technology and economic growth would be supreme, and in which capital would still be concentrated enough that individuals and groups could invest heavily in new spinoffs or corporate offspring. Seen in the context of these issues, Turnbull's vision of economic change might be an intermediate step that would pave the way for a system of complete equality and limited, universal ownership.

The first question we should ask, though, is this: Do we have thirty years to convert our present system into Turnbull's vision, which is still only a halfway house from our current economic prison to the free society we would become? The answer, I fear, is that we may not have even ten years. Time is not on our side in this matter.

The fundamental question of management theory is: What links individuals together in cooperative endeavor? The answer, according to the contemporary management orthodoxy, is self-interest—the raw egoism of Hobbes and Mandeville, refurbished in chic, modern, linguistic garb. . . . All organizational behavior is summarized in the inelegant phrase, "What's in it for me?"

—David K. Hart,
"The Sympathetic
Organization"

8

Competition Restrained
By a Higher Good

The suggested changes to our ownership tradition discussed in the preceding chapter are entirely structural in nature. And although structural changes are necessary both to prevent economic suicide and to bring our economy into harmony with our political and social patterns, structural changes alone are not sufficient. Altering the structure of our economy without somehow modifying the habitual patterns of human thought and interaction would be similar to buying new computer hardware, but running the same old virus-infected software. In essence, as individuals we have been operating within the structures and patterns of unbridled capitalism for so long that even if we suddenly found ourselves on a completely different playing field, most of us would go right on behaving as the system has always rewarded us for behaving.

There is a moral aspect to this question of economics that

we must deal with on an individual, rather than a structural, level. Implementing a new economic structure with new rules and restrictions would of course reward individuals for behaving in new ways, but some behavioral patterns are quite hard to break—and you can't legislate everything, morality in particular. Consequently, we must develop a new economic rationale, a moral argument, if you will, to support the types of behavior that must accompany the necessary structural changes. This moral argument must address two related issues: *self-interest* and *competition*.

Why We Need a Guiding Philosophy

In *The Worldly Philosophers*, Robert Heilbroner explains in some detail why we have had political, moral, and social philosophers for millennia, but economists (or worldly philosophers) only in the past few hundred years. There are, he says, three basic approaches to ensuring the survival of the human race. First, society can organize itself by tradition. In essence, people serve particular functions in society because their fathers did, or because they are limited by their class or caste to certain types of labor. Second, authoritarian government can ensure that tasks get done by assigning people to do them, whether they want to or not. Neither of these approaches to ensuring survival required any kind of economic philosophy. Only the third alternative demanded an accompanying rationale. And this third alternative was "an astonishing arrangement in which society assured its own continuance by allowing each individual to do exactly as he saw fit—provided he followed a central guiding rule. The arrangement was called the 'market system,' and the rule was deceptively simple: each should do what was to his best monetary advantage" (Heilbroner, 1986, 20-21).

This third arrangement was not unrelated to the social and

political philosophies of classical liberalism, suggesting that individuals were more important than the traditionally authoritarian institutions to which they belonged. Liberty, self-rule, justice, equality, private property, happiness—all these ideas added momentum to the great change from traditional or command systems to a free-market economy. "No mistake about it," says Heilbroner, "the travail was over and the market system had been born. The problem of survival was henceforth to be solved neither by custom nor by command, but by the free action of profit-seeking men bound together only by the market itself. . . . The idea [however] needed a philosophy" (ibid., 38). And philosophies abounded. Starting with Adam Smith and continuing on to the present day, great and not so great thinkers have put forward their ideas on how to best order and justify this new system. "Out of the *mêlée* of contradictory rationalizations one thing alone stood clear: man insisted on some sort of intellectual ordering to help him understand the world in which he lived. The harsh and disconcerting economic world loomed ever more important" (ibid., 41).

Indeed, economic matters loom more and more important as time passes, for the simple reason that our economic system must continually rationalize its very existence. That third alternative requires a philosophy, a justification, because when push comes to shove it is in conflict with the political, social, and moral philosophies of classical liberalism, the foundation of our Western way of life. This third arrangement for ensuring the continuance of human society is based solely upon the principle of self-interest, a principle that, when isolated, is at odds with the political theories, social ideals, and moral principles that have shaped our Western world.

Self-interest, however, is too problematic as a sole motivator of people in a community. When made the guiding rule, when unchecked by social constraints, political intervention, or moral concerns, monetary self-interest leads inevitably to centralized power, authoritarian structures, and command systems. In other words, without a motive higher than self-interest to guide or at least temper it, the third alternative inevitably collapses back into some form of the second alternative, and the individual ends up again at the mercy of arbitrary authority. For a while our political system, our social objectives, and our good moral sense held this contrarious economic motivator at bay, but in the end the strain was too great. Something had to give, and self-interested economics had too much momentum, too much appeal. What we need desperately today is a fourth approach, an approach that goes beyond custom, command, and self-interest, an approach consistent with our political, social, and moral heritage.

Republican Disinterest

Self-interest is actually a moral question, not just a value-neutral economic motor that is supposed to drive the mindless machinery of the free market. Indeed, self-interest is a very troubling moral question, for an economic system based on this principle creates almost irresistible incentives for people to behave in patently immoral ways.

Who would argue that we must be a moral people in order for self-government to work? This is what some would call a "no-brainer." The freer we are, the greater a burden we as individual citizens must bear in creating a society of order and justice. Republicanism, succeeding monarchy as the dominant political system, "put an enormous burden on individuals," says Gordon Wood. "They were expected to suppress their private wants and interests and develop disinterestedness—the term the eighteenth century most often used as a synonym for civic virtue. . . . Dr. Johnson defined disinterest as being 'superior to regard of private advantage; not influenced by private profit.' We today have lost most of this older meaning. Even some educated people now use 'disinterested' as a synonym for 'uninterested,' meaning indifferent or unconcerned" (Wood, 1991, 104-5). Disinterest, however, is actually the exact opposite of self-interest.

"Republics," Wood continues, "demanded far more morally from their citizens than monarchies did of their subjects. In monarchies each man's desire to do what was right in his own eyes could be restrained by fear or force." In republics, the only effective restraint on self-interest and private gratification is the sense among citizens that they must often sacrifice personal advantage for the public welfare. It is indeed ironic that self-interest—the one force that Wood identifies as needing to be restrained if a republic is to hold together—is the *only* force that traditional economic theory proposes as a social adhesive. This is not only a highly illogical thesis, it is also a disturbingly immoral philosophy.

What we have in modern America, then, is a form of government that requires a disinterested citizenry and an economic system founded on the principle of self-interest—a perfect mismatch. And, unfortunately, the economy is in control. To correct this problem, as I have already suggested, we cannot merely tell people to become disinterested. All the incentives in the present system encourage the exact opposite behavior. What we need is a fundamental change in the structure of the economy, so that our economic system actually encourages disinterested action. But we also need a higher ideal than self-interest to bind us together, for self-interest, even though it does cause us to "do business" with one another, also creates too many impediments to true economic and societal health.

Lip Service

The escalating height and frequency of the hurdles economic America requires companies to jump if they want to stay in the race puts immense pressure on them to increase their productivity and develop innovative new technologies. A very natural consequence of this pressure, within a system that enshrines self-interest, is for companies to become, over time, increasingly and hostilely competitive. American companies have always felt the need for, even thrived on, fierce competition, but as the growth spiral steepens and accelerates, making it harder for companies to climb to the next level, their perceived need to compete will intensify dramatically. In our twentieth-century mercenary marketplace you either eat or get eaten. Consequently, most companies nowadays focus *primarily* on beating their competitors and enlarging their bottom lines, rather than providing a service to society.

I used to ask the students in my management classes at the university, just to keep a finger on the pulse of their attitudes and misconceptions, what the purpose of a business is. I always asked this out of the blue, without any sort of preamble to bias their replies. And without exception, their first answer was, "To make a profit." Rarely, even when I dug a little deeper, did they bring up the radical notion that businesses exist to provide a service to society. These were juniors and seniors in the business curriculum, and they had learned their lessons well. They were prepared for life in corporate America, or, as they called it, "the real world." This "real world," however, is anything but real. It is both inconsistent with the values of the American Dream and inherently illogical.

I remember reading the account of one business consultant who asked a group of high-level executives the same question. Their answer was identical to that of my students. They said their businesses existed to make a profit. This wise consultant then asked them how their drug and prostitution operations were doing. The executives were, of course, astonished at this request. "I just assumed," he answered, "if you were in business to make money, that you'd be involved in the most profitable kind of business." To bypass the best opportunities would be both inefficient and contrary to the stated purpose of their companies. These executives suddenly understood that their business activities were restricted by deeper purposes that they had perhaps not yet fathomed. And so it is with almost all companies.

Businesses today, for the most part, are so caught up in beating the competition, expanding their operations, and making a profit that they are either oblivious to or, at best, pay lip service to the idea of serving society. They are anything but disinterested. Corporate mission statements and hordes of management gurus notwithstanding, businesses have become ends unto themselves rather than instruments for achieving a greater societal good. And their recruits from the business schools already know which side their bread's buttered on.

The problem with this acute management myopia is that on the practical, everyday side of the ledger the larger question of economics is ignored, thus focusing all the attention and resources of corporate America on the grand ideal of making a buck. The direct consequences of corporate America's short-sightedness and misdirected energies are not trivial.

Because businesses and other institutions are not knit together in common purpose by an openly acknowledged concern for the greater good of society, but operate primarily on the principles of self-interest and self-perpetuation, the competitive climate in America has become one of hostility and aggression rather than cooperation and fair play. Because of this prevailing climate, modern businesses and business people are necessarily caught up in a brutal fight for survival. They must not only survive the inherent illogic of the system, they must also survive head-on confrontations with competitors who wouldn't blink an eye at putting them in their economic grave.

Survival is what twentieth-century American capitalism is all about, not service, not quality, not human development. Companies focus on quality, not for quality's sake, but in order to survive. They emphasize service, not for the customer's sake, but to increase market share. They create more humane workplaces, not because of their belief that workers in a free society *deserve* to more fully develop and express their talents and ingenuity, but because they can no longer compete in today's demanding marketplace without intelligent, motivated, highly trained workers. At the bottom of American capitalism is the competition for survival—survival of the fittest. And as Abraham Maslow points out, when our survival is threatened, we are simply incapable of paying attention to higher needs and concerns.

Who Really Believes in Unfettered Competition?

Unfettered competition, most free-market advocates insist, is the most necessary component of a successful economic system. And the most convincing argument supporting this assertion just happens to be communism. Ask any capitalist if unrestricted competition is good, and the answer will be, "Of course competition is good. All you have to do to see this clearly is to look at communism, a system that removes competition from economic endeavor."

Any capitalist would tell you that competition is necessary in order to achieve quality, efficiency, and variety. Communism does not achieve these three desirable results, but is that because communism lacks the competitive forces of capitalism?

Perhaps it lacks a great many other things too. Unfettered competition does indeed fuel the fires of quality, efficiency, and variety, but the reasons for achieving these ends are all wrong. Wouldn't it be better to achieve them for the right reasons, for a higher purpose, such as the good of society and the full preservation of choice in the marketplace?

The conservatives, in particular, talk a good game when it comes to unregulated competition. In fact, given the opposing view, their talk makes a good deal of sense. They pledge allegiance to the banner of laissez-faire capitalism, all in the name of freedom. But do they walk their talk? Do they really believe their own words? The evidence here, I'm afraid, is against them. As David Barash explains:

> We are supposed to believe that conservatives believe in the virtues of competition, tooth and nail, dog eat dog, and may the best man win. . . . But do they really believe in such a free-for-all? Consider the Lockheed and Savings and Loan bailouts, or the various and numerous forms of "corporate socialism" whereby government provides special benefits and tax breaks to large corporations, especially those engaged in military contracting. What conservatives really prefer is competition among the nonrich, the wage earners, the smaller and less well established . . . especially since out of this competitive fray generally come lower wages and a more docile workforce. (Barash, 1992, 176)

Many people claim to believe in unhindered competition, but when push comes to shove, we discover that they'd actually prefer to have the government step in and ensure their success and prosperity, rather than having to "earn" it (and possibly lose it) in the mercenary marketplace they extol. It is only certain classes of individuals, apparently, who should be unprotected from the hostile, predatory environment. So who really does believe in a totally free market? Perhaps no one.

Both individuals and businesses usually believe in free

competition only to the degree that they feel they can win. If I were scheduled to play Andre Agassi at tennis, for instance, I wouldn't be so gung-ho about competition. Self-interest, as one might expect, lies at the heart of the competition issue. If unfettered competition is in our best interest, we're for it; if, on the other hand, our competitors are in a position of strength, we immediately want the rules changed. Sure, I'll take on Andre— if he wears leg chains, a straitjacket, and holds the racquet in his teeth.

A Better Metaphor

Three metaphors have often been used to define our win-lose competitive system: (1) the athletic contest or "game," (2) war, which bears striking similarities to sports, and (3) the jungle. One major problem with these win-lose metaphors is that they all serve as excuses for not creating a system in which our unique American ideals can be practiced. They disavow any higher goal that should focus and mold our competitiveness.

The game metaphor is inappropriate, for life is not a game. Food and shelter and health care and education should not be the prize for winning a contest. The war metaphor is also improper, for doing battle over the necessities of life, or even the luxuries, is barbarous. We are a society, we claim to be civilized, and we must either unite and thrive or splinter, decline, and die as a society. The jungle metaphor is perhaps most repulsive, for human beings are not simply members of the animal kingdom. Our intelligence, creativity, self-awareness, advanced communication skills, preservation of history, and capacity to rise above instinct and exercise reason and compassion set us apart from other animals. Why, then, should we be satisfied with economic relationships based on a metaphor that applies better to lions or sharks or raccoons? Why can't we adopt a metaphor that places our economic interaction on a par with our social and political aspirations?

What we need is a better metaphor to guide us in economic endeavors. Consider, perhaps, the orchestra metaphor. There is indeed competition between the violinists in an orchestra. They all desire to occupy the first chair. But this competition is not an unfettered, totally self-interested, win-lose type of competition. The last thing any serious violinist wants is for another violinist to play wrong notes, for this would reflect on the whole orchestra. A higher good governs the competition. Each violinist wants the orchestra—and, hence, all of its parts—to play superbly, flawlessly. But each violinist wants to be recognized as the best—not because others foul up, but because he or she is simply more excellent than the others. This healthy competition rests on the idea of being considered the best of the best. And it is all possible because a greater common good, a higher ideal governs the competition and binds the players together.

The only way we can have this type of competition in our economic pursuits is for us as citizens to recognize a higher ideal. If we can learn to view the American Dream as something more than an economic game of grabs, perhaps we can experience a quality of life and social excellence that has eluded us.

Free Competition Leads to Authoritarianism

Unfortunately, however, we do not yet live in such a society. We live in a system that permits unlimited capital ownership, and we behave according to the win-lose metaphors. And it is not surprising that this type of mercenary competition carries its own inherent flaw: The freely competitive marketplace becomes less competitive over time, the inevitable result being an increase in inequality—in other words, a swift departure from a central goal of the American Dream.

David Korten explains that "a competitive market is competitive only when there are enough buyers and sellers that each has many alternatives. However, by its nature, untempered competition creates winners and losers. Winners tend to grow in economic power while losers disappear. The bigger the winners, the more difficult it is for new entrants to gain a foothold. Market control tends to concentrate in a few firms, so that the conditions for competition are eroded" (Korten, 1991-92, 26-27).

The longer the free market remains totally free, the less competitive it becomes. This is inevitable, but *to say that it becomes less competitive does not mean that it becomes more cooperative.* On the contrary, as power concentrates, only the most successful predators thrive, and the resulting imbalance fosters autocratic rather than democratic relationships. Unrestricted competitive economies tend quite naturally toward authoritarian systems.

Because untempered competition destroys the competitive marketplace, there must be some sort of restraint placed on competition. And we have two choices. We can either change the structure of our system to make cooperation and fair play more attractive and then bridle our own behavior by following common sense and proven moral truth or we can pass laws and regulations to bind our hands. The latter, which we are now pursuing with a vengeance, is really no choice at all, for you can't legislate morality. You can't enforce it either. When internal moral checks and structural barriers to immoral behavior are nonexistent, no amount of enforcement on either Wall Street or Main Street will stop individuals and institutions from finding loopholes in the system, from behaving like predators. If we want a mercenary marketplace where competition is virtually nonexistent, then let's make no changes in the status quo. But if we are even half serious about creating a moral, fair, cooperative marketplace, then we need both structural limits and internal moral barriers to protect us from the abuses that we've grown accustomed to. '

Benevolence

In a significant paper, titled "The Sympathetic Organization," David K. Hart points to a philosophically sound path that would lead us to the type of economic relationships we need. He argues convincingly that "human nature [has] not one, but two, primordial aspects: the need to love self (self-love) and the need to love others (benevolence)" (Hart, 1988b, 68). A major problem with modern capitalism is that it has enthroned self-love ("What's in it for me?") and abandoned benevolence. Hart insists that this organizational neglect of a fundamental human need has created a society in which individuals are alienated not only from one another, but from themselves and their work. "Alienation results when an individual is separated from something *essential* to the development of his or her full human potential. It is not, then, just a minor psychological dyspepsia, but rather the spiritual sickness that comes with the ruination of one's life possibilities. Our modern age experiences it through the soul-destroying entanglements of modern organizational life" (ibid., 71).

Organizations, in essence, dehumanize individuals by treating them as functions. "In modern organizations, individuals are linked to other individuals in artificial relationships defined solely by the organizational mission" (Hart, 1988b, 77). Friendship and benevolence are not only unnecessary in such an environment, but often harmful to organizational objectives.

"The management orthodoxy," Hart concludes, "is not only incorrect but unendurable. Based upon a mutilated version of the whole self, the orthodoxy reduces individuals to their organizational functions and estranges them from the rewards of their work. Work is devalued into an instrumental activity valuable only for what it contributes to organizational goals. It has no intrinsic meaning. The individual's labor is a commodity and this makes the individual a commodity also" (Hart, 1988b, 87). Human beings who are treated as commodities cannot reach their full human potential, nor can they become truly happy.

What I wish to establish by inserting a portion of Hart's argument at this point is not merely that the absence of benevolence and the abundance of alienation in modern society are negatives that we should correct. In the context of this book, the relevant point is that self-interest's domination in modern capitalism is not mere coincidence. Self-interest and unlimited ownership are products of each other. Self-interest, of course, lies behind the desire to accumulate unlimited capital, but unlimited capital ownership also begets greater self-interest.

What I have proposed thus far is that we abolish unlimited capital ownership. This is a structural change. But if we change the structure without also correcting the moral and behavioral flaw it promotes, then the untempered self-interest rampant in society will pervert and perhaps destroy the new structure we attempt to introduce.

What we must undertake is not just an economic reformation; we must attack the very roots of our un-American economic system. We will be unsuccessful in this venture, however, unless we can embrace a higher goal than "What's in it for me?" and unless we can restore that part of our nature that unrestricted capitalism has taught us to ignore: benevolence.

Restrained Competition

The reason for both restructuring the parameters of capital ownership and encouraging individuals to adopt benevolence as a guiding star in their economic dealings is to curb the competitive nature of our economy. As discussed earlier, the most compelling argument for a highly competitive economy is that competition is responsible for all the things that make our lives comfortable, secure, and healthy. Without competition, we are told, people are not motivated to succeed, and there is little impetus behind technological advancement. Competition, because it pits one individual or company against another in a struggle for survival, yields a never-ending stream of new products, each intended to give its producer an advantage over "the competition."

While I admit that competition does spur technological growth, and that the by-products of corporate warfare have benefitted society in many ways, I have come to two other beliefs: first, that competition has also brought us the waste and inefficiency of planned obsolescence, the curse of a decimated environment, artificial growth that is becoming a straitjacket rather than a liberating force, and an economy based on adversarial relationships rather than cooperative ones; and second, that competition is *not* the only impetus for improving the human condition.

Indeed, I submit that a noncompetitive environment would actually free people to be *more innovative, more creative, and more directly motivated to make life better for one another*. Regardless of the competitive or noncompetitive nature of their environment, human beings have an innate desire to improve their individual and collective condition. And in a noncompetitive environment the risks of failure that deter all but the most daring innovators would be gone. In short, if we removed the rewards for self-interested innovation, I believe more people would be inclined to share Ben Franklin's attitude and motives for bettering the lives of their neighbors:

To avoid or overcome the perpetual problems caused by miscalculations of self-interest, Benjamin Franklin chose the course of modesty and disinterestedness as a means for progressing. True, Franklin wanted to succeed in his business and he worked hard to do so. . . . But in all his endeavors, his objectives were to *do* good and to *be* useful as opposed to getting rich or gathering honors. His emphasis was on contributing rather than obtaining; on giving rather than receiving. Strange as it may seem, it was Franklin's "indifference to the things of this world" that unleashed his full creative powers. . . .

Benjamin Franklin was one of those rare individuals who had it within his power to become immensely wealthy, but who declined the opportunity to do so. To his mother he had written that he would rather have it said of him that he had lived usefully than that he had died rich. When his business attained a level to assure him of financial independence he turned his interests to science and government. Believing "That, as we enjoy great advantages from the inventions of others, we should be glad of an opportunity to serve others by any invention of ours; and this we should do freely and generously," he made no effort to patent or profit from any of his inventions. The Franklin stove alone could have made him a fortune, but he chose not to patent it, and printed the plans for it in his own newspaper. (Franklin, 1990, 115, 158-59)

A noncompetitive system based on limited capital ownership and benevolent behavior would breed this sort of outlook on life. It is our current system and its rewards that work to prevent this sympathetic way of living, which to varying degrees lies dormant in the hearts of men and women everywhere. A noncompetitive system, in which people didn't have to fight and scratch for their "just due," would unlock many of these latent qualities and put them into action. Large authoritarian organizations, on the other hand, must manipulate or force creativity and innovation to the surface.

If people were freed from the desperate craving to secure their future and the perceived necessity of acquiring more than they actually need, they might be surprisingly inclined, even eager, to focus their energies on assisting their fellow men and women—and find great happiness in doing so. In such a society, "What's in it for me?" would become obsolete thinking.

*Those who have money to lend are in
a favored position to obtain still more wealth,
ultimately at the expense of those who receive
their income from wages or the sale of produce
and handicrafts. Pervasive usury and speculation
tend to destroy the social fabric because they
reward the clever and penalize those afflicted
with the old-fashioned virtues of thrift,
productive skills, and industry. . . . Because of
the inherent tendency of the system to favor the
lender over the debtor, national debt tends to
outrun national income. Interest payments
on national debt tend to outrun gross national
product. . . . Total public and private debt in
the United States has been rising over the past
three decades at a rate far higher than inflation,
population increase, or real economic ouput—
something over 10 percent per year.*

—Willis Harman,
"Whatever Happened
to Usury?"

9

The Developing Economy

If the main points asserted thus far in this book are true—if progress, the keystone to liberal and conservative programs, is an inherently dead-end socioeconomic philosophy; if modern capitalism's consumer-driven growth spiral has steepened and accelerated to the degree that we can climb no higher without inflicting severe damage on both our economy and our ecology; if our out-of-control economy has subjugated our political and social ideals—then we must ask ourselves one question and only one question: *Is it possible to provide for the physical needs and reasonable wants of our society with an economic system not based on goalless progress and not dependent on endless growth?*

Theoretically, we should be able to provide for everyone's needs and reasonable wants with a relatively static economy. The only reason why endless growth is necessary in the capitalist system is simply that it is the mechanism by which the system works. Without growth, capitalism deteriorates. But the growth imperative causes some rather serious side effects, one of which is the tendency to confuse both money and debt with wealth.

Wealth and Debt

The relationship between wealth and debt is fairly direct, yet not particularly easy to fathom. If I own debt—if, for instance, I have loaned $1,000 to a friend—I might well assume that I still own the equivalent in real wealth, but such is not the case. Debt, if you will, is disembodied wealth, wealth that has died and gone to heaven and given up certain physical limitations. And in this fact lies a great danger of our growth-driven economic system. Because real wealth is subject to real, physical limits, it cannot grow exponentially, as we desire it to. We therefore settle for the illusion of growth and convert our real wealth into something else, something symbolic that can and does grow exponentially: debt.

As mentioned in an earlier chapter, if we do not consume or use up real wealth, it perishes on its own. We can't store enough of it to satisfy our lifelong needs. The only way we can make today's wealth fulfill tomorrow's needs is to lend it to others, put them in our debt, and persuade them to pay us back over time (with interest, of course). One negative consequence of turning wealth into debt, however, is that debt, being nonconcrete and imaginary, tends to expand regularly and indefinitely, while the wealth it symbolizes cannot.

Daly and Cobb present a curious metaphor to illustrate why debt is so much more desirable than wealth. Two pigs, they say, is a quantity of real "wealth that can be seen and touched. But minus two pigs, debt, is an imaginary negative magnitude with no physical dimension. One could as easily have a thousand negative pigs as two." In fact, a thousand negative pigs is far preferable to two negative pigs, because it means someone owes you a thousand pigs instead of just two. "Compound interest or exponential growth of negative pigs presents no problem. But exponential growth of positive pigs soon leads to bedlam and ruin." Because negative pigs are so much more convenient to own, "the ruling passion of individuals in a modern economy is to convert wealth into debt in order to derive a permanent future income from it" (Daly and Cobb, [1989] 1994, 423).

This is the heart of capitalism. Learn how to create and possess a surplus of real wealth, then convert that wealth first into money and finally into debt by lending (or investing) it, charge compound interest, reap a perpetual return on it, and live off this return.

The fallacy here lies in the idea that income in an economy will always be large enough to offset the demands of an ever-increasing debt. "But the idea that all people can live off the interest of their mutual indebtedness is just another perpetual motion scheme—a vulgar delusion on a grand scale" (ibid., 424).

In reality, only the minority earns significant interest, and the majority pays it. But under the assumption of exponential growth of debt (compound interest), the difference between what the majority owes and what it is able to pay steadily widens. Debt grows exponentially, but new real wealth, which common laborers must repeatedly create to pay the interest on their borrowings, does not. This produces a predicament in which we never really can pay off all our debts. We can never produce enough actual growth in wealth to keep up with the exponential growth of our debts. We just roll them over, and eventually we end up borrowing to pay the interest on them, which is nothing more than a giant, legalized Ponzi scheme.

"Clearly," writes Willis Harman, "to think of the many trillions of dollars of federal, municipal, corporate, and private debt in the United States alone ever being repaid is sheer fantasy.

Since by far the greatest part of the money supply consists of currency or bank credit that has been borrowed into existence, it is impossible for people, in the aggregate, to get out of debt. To do so would require the repayment to primary lenders of more money than there ever is in existence" (Harman, 1992, 20).

"The 'solution' to the debt crisis offered by the orthodox economist," explain Daly and Cobb, "has been a further dose of growth. The way to grow is to invest, and the way to invest is to borrow. The solution to the debt is to increase the debt! Just why it is believed this new debt will be used so much more productively than the older debt is never explained" (Daly and Cobb, [1989] 1994, 232).

Daly and Cobb conclude that the resulting explosion of debt will lead inevitably to defensive actions by borrowers to repudiate or reject that debt. These defensive actions may include inflation, bankruptcy, confiscatory taxation, fraud, or outright theft. These are socially and economically destructive actions, and yet they are also the inevitable fruit of compound interest, which we deem normal and acceptable.

The logical solution to this dilemma is really rather simple. Since exponential growth of real wealth is physically impossible, we must tie the money supply more closely to wealth to keep it from expanding needlessly. How do we do this? According to Daly and Cobb, we do it by eliminating any growth in money that does not accompany an expansion of real wealth. Money now expands without regard to real wealth because commercial banks are required to hold only a fraction (about 3 percent) of their demand deposits as reserves. This permits them, theoretically, to "loan money into existence" at the rate of about 33 times the amount of demand deposits they receive. The only way to restrict such monetary (and debt) growth is to require a 100 percent reserve ratio on demand deposits.

A 100 percent reserve ratio would produce two corrective effects. First, it would prevent commercial banks from creating both money and debt out of thin air. Only government would then have the power to increase the money supply. And, second, it would significantly curtail the exponential growth (or compounding) of debt, because there would be so much less of it. The debt created under these restrictions would represent real wealth that had been converted to liens on future income, rather than debt that banks had created as if by magic. The return on such debt would also more accurately reflect the limited physical growth of real wealth.

This recommendation has great merit, for it would bring the money system more in line with the realities that govern the physical economy. In essence, it would keep debt from expanding beyond our capacity to repay it. It would also put a damper on exponential monetary growth, which encourages a particularly insidious, though popular, fallacy: that real wealth can grow as rapidly and consistently as debt.

Free Trade and the International Movement of Capital

Exponential growth of money and debt creates unrealistic expectations for similar growth in real wealth, which in turn puts immense pressure on short-term profits and return on investment. If I can reap a 15 percent return on speculative monetary transactions that have nothing to do with the actual production and consumption of goods, why should I settle for the 7 percent return I could earn by investing in new plant and equipment for my own or someone else's business? Thus, to attract capital, businesses must offer a competitive return, which often means that they search the world over for the lowest-cost production opportunity. Frequently, this means closing up shop at home and building production facilities in Korea or Malaysia or Namibia or Russia, where wages are significantly lower and the potential returns are greater.

This brings up the question of free trade, which nearly all economists subscribe to. Free trade between nations, we ought to understand, is not analogous to free trade within a single nation. The difference is that free trade *within* a nation encourages the unrestricted movement of both capital and labor, while free trade *between* nations brings only the unrestricted movement of capital. Labor, for the most part, stays put, which results not in mutual benefit to both nations, but significantly lower wages in the country that loses capital.

When we talk of free trade, we are talking about the unrestricted movement of capital across national boundaries. Such movement, of course, creates trade deficits and surpluses. "Balanced trade and capital immobility," explain Daly and Cobb, "are two sides of the same coin. The way a country borrows in real terms is to import more than it exports" (ibid., 230). In recent decades, of course, the United States has run up a staggering trade debt. What this means is that immense amounts of capital have moved from America to other nations.

No economist would maintain that this large trade imbalance can continue to expand forever. At some point, capital will have to start flowing in the opposite direction to bring the account back into balance. But for this to happen, wages and benefits of American workers will have to fall to globally competitive (Third-World) levels. Dramatic shifts in the exchange rate may account for much of the equalizing that must take place, but the end result is the same: the living standard of American workers will drop significantly. Daly and Cobb remind us, however, that "this does not mean that the standard of living of all Americans will decline. One segment of American society lives from capital rather than labor. The freedom of such capital to move internationally offers unparalleled opportunities for profit. The growth of the gap between the rich and poor will continue" (ibid., 225).

Basically, what free trade means is that the capitalist or independent class can ask the laboring or dependent class to reduce its standard of living to Third-World levels, while the capitalists grow more wealthy from the abundance of opportunity afforded by a low-wage global economy.

This is where our addiction to exponential growth is taking us. As long as capitalists are free to invest where they will, without regard to national and community concerns, such as balanced trade, decent wages, and job security, we will continue to become an increasingly fractured, impoverished, and debt-laden society. This is the road to crisis of one sort or another.

Under current ownership arrangements, the only way to prevent the scenario painted above is to require a balance in trade and, hence, immobile capital. Balanced trade, of course, would require some kind of governmental control over trade, but who, we might ask, really wants free, unrestricted trade? Only those who stand to gain the most from the free movement of capital, the capitalists. As things now stand, it is not nations that trade with each other, but individuals and businesses within those nations, and free trade has made those individuals and businesses unaccountable to the larger community from which they have severed themselves and which they are damaging with their self-interested actions. Balanced trade means that nations would still be able to trade with each other, but their trade would not drain capital from any society and impoverish its citizens.

Let's look briefly at the foregoing argument in conjunction with the structural changes discussed in Chapter 7. If businesses belonged not to individual capitalists or to groups of distant stockholders who seek merely an optimum return on their investment, but to the workers themselves, would the owners choose to close down their workplace, put themselves out of work, build factories in foreign countries, and pay low-wage laborers to do their work for them? We must admit, I believe, that in a system of worker-owners the incentive to do so vanishes, particularly if tariffs are established to protect American worker-owned businesses from foreign competitors who pay subsistence-level wages. Again, it is not really our trade laws that are the fundamental problem; it is the structure of our economy, how we permit ourselves to own and generate capital. Immobile capital and balanced trade, it can be argued, would be natural results of the structural changes I recommended in earlier chapters. How else can we expect to reverse the increasing inequality and economic mayhem that the current system is forcing upon us?

These arguments, as well as those presented in Chapters 3 and 4, suggest that we must look for an alternative to this insane assumption of endless, exponential growth. But what would a system not dependent on growth look like? I don't have all the answers, but the following ideas might at least point us in the right direction.

Growth Versus Development

Herman Daly explains the difference between economic growth and economic development: "'To grow' means to increase in size by the . . . assimilation of material. 'Growth' therefore means a quantitative increase in . . . the physical dimensions of the economy. 'To develop' means to expand or realize the potentialities of; to bring gradually to a . . . better state. 'Development' therefore means [a] qualitative improvement . . . . A growing economy is getting bigger; a developing economy is getting better. An economy can therefore develop without growing, or grow without developing" (Daly, 1990, 116-17).

An economy driven by the perceived need to grow exponentially is full of superfluous products and nonproducts (purely financial instruments) that the average American never really asked for nor would miss terribly if they were to disappear. It is also full of inherently expensive or wasteful products. A growth-driven economy feeds ultimately on the perpetual transformation of luxury into necessity and is propelled by the dual engines of self-interest and exponential debt. A developing economy, on the other hand, might offer fewer products, but those products would more accurately incorporate the actual costs to society of both their production and consumption. A developing economy would certainly be more localized, more community-oriented, more attuned to quality of life than to standard of living.

Paul Hawken offers several compelling suggestions on how to design an *economical* economy, one that is inherently *conservative* (not wasteful) in both its production and consumption. One recommendation he makes is to conserve energy by designing products that can be "disassembled and remanufactured." Such products will require more labor, but will use less energy and produce less waste. "This is one example," he says, "of how, in the restorative economy, productivity can go *down*, employment up, and profits increase" (Hawken, 1993, 69). This runs contrary to conventional economic logic.

Hawken also recommends the assessing of green fees, taxes on production that essentially make companies pay for the costs they now so effectively externalize—pollution, increasing medical problems, depletion of nonrenewable resources, and so on. Such fees would discourage businesses from producing products that are frivolous (cars that go twice the speed limit), dangerous (cigarettes), and dirty (carbon-based energy). They would encourage products that are useful, safe, and clean. And, more important, they would teach businesses something they should already know—that their products have a higher purpose than the generation of profit (at any cost) and the creation of growth (for the sake of growth).

A non-growth-based system would have many features lacking in our current economy, the most important of which would be the presence of a higher, unifying social purpose, an emphasis on creating a good life for everyone without consuming the world we must live in or impoverishing those who don't happen to own capital. Such a system will be possible only if we remove the existing incentives for unlimited growth, which means, essentially, discouraging or even deterring the formation of enormous, impersonal, capital-driven corporations and encouraging the generation of small, employee-owned, service-oriented, society- and environment-sensitive businesses.

The new economic system, if it is to achieve its objectives, must not only be in harmony with our political heritage, it must be administered by a moral people, and it must also tackle the social questions that liberals and conservatives, like a matched pair of blind eyes, seem unable to see. This is a monumental challenge, but if we do not accept it and instead continue on in our current insanity, we shall see our great American experiment come to an abrupt and premature end.

The Nongrowth Economy

If we are able somehow to avert economic disaster and convert to a system of limited, universal ownership, our economy will take on a radically new shape and direction. For starters, the imperative for both the economy and individual companies to grow without limits will effectively be negated. The need for companies to extract excessive short-term profits will largely vanish, as will the incentives for companies to pursue relentless growth by infusing outside capital. It would be impossible for businesses to "go public," because publicly held corporations will have been abolished. Corporate takeovers and the resulting debt burden and wholesale firing of employees will also be a thing of the past. Workers will not be laid off in droves, because they will no longer be "employees"—mere property of the business—and will not be at the mercy of powerful corporate owners or professional executives. Workers will no longer be just part of the bottom line: in a very real sense, *they will be the company*.

The incentives in a limited-ownership economy would lead inexorably away from multinational conglomerates that produce thousands of products in locations all over the globe and would encourage small to medium-sized businesses that produce just one or a handful of related products. Companies would be prone to focus primarily on serving society (producing something truly useful) rather than on the bottom line. Taking on enormous sums of debt and selling equity in an all-out effort to accumulate capital and pursue market share for the sake of becoming the biggest and strongest (and therefore most secure) will be antiquated business practices, and eventually we shall recognize these tactics as the immensely wasteful activities they are.

These smaller, community-oriented companies would also be more sensitive to environmental issues, because they would be owned by the same people who drink the water, breathe the air, and live in the immediate environment affected by the company's production techniques. Such community-based companies are inherently more sensitive to environmental issues than immense conglomerates whose plants are nowhere near the homes of the distant executives who make decisions that impact local environments.

The growth of worker-owned companies would also be self-limiting, just like all natural systems. Without the ability either to acquire other businesses or to take on the exponential growth requirements of public stock offerings, companies would grow as all natural systems do—gradually and with an inherent sense of balanced efficiency. The huge, superfluous support structure that holds up the actual production and consumption of capitalism would be largely unneeded, and more people would engage in the actual creation of something useful. What this means is that most Americans would have to work far fewer hours to produce and distribute the products society needs and wants.

An economy based on limited ownership would also furnish less incentive to perpetuate rampant consumerism. Instead of creating demand by wielding huge advertising budgets and planning rapid and repeated product obsolescence, companies would respond more directly with the goods and services people really need and want. Producers would be looking for permanence and a secure market rather than an all-out storming of the marketplace with new products that only a rapidly expanding economy can afford and that must be replaced faster and faster as the overall growth spiral accelerates and steepens.

A technological explosion such as we have experienced in the past few decades would be inconsistent with this type of economy. New technological developments would be driven by neither a frenzied, artificial consumerism nor rabid competitiveness, but by actual societal needs and sensible wants. Hence, we may not have computers that can take verbal commands and run our households for us or disposable cameras or four hundred digitally transmitted TV channels, but perhaps we will devise new methods of producing food and shelter and clothing and transportation that restore rather than waste the environment.

We would see the greatest change, however, in the end of

gluttonous growth driven by self-interest and exponentially expanding debt. Cutthroat competition would give way to a more cooperative atmosphere, in which a higher, unifying goal would govern economic transactions. Since I would be able to own only so much, it would no longer be in my best interest to put my competitors out of business. What good would it do me? I can eat only one lunch a day. It would be stupid and vindictive of me to steal or destroy someone else's lunch, just because I can't eat it on top of my own. In the long run such predatory acts would only weaken society.

Of course the market mechanism would still be in place, although governed by reasonable limits, and there would be both relatively wealthy businesses and others with more modest earnings, but the vast gulf between the rich and the poor would fade away, for that gulf is created by the fact that certain individuals can acquire unlimited capital, which gives them the power to buy the time and energy of those who have no capital. This new economic system, you might say, would be a truer form of capitalism, for everyone who was healthy and even minimally motivated would own capital, and in reasonably equal portions.

An economic system that mandated limited, universal ownership, although still susceptible to many of the same abuses our current system permits, would nonetheless eliminate most of the incentives that lead people to behave as predators and mercenaries rather than as cooperative members of a society with an overarching common goal of happiness and peaceful prosperity. Such a system would be subject, however, to the same condition the Founding Fathers recognized for our republican democracy—namely, that it will work only for a moral and religious people. And in that area, although changing our economic incentives would help, we still have much work to do.

Predators and Parasites

Our current system has shown a great propensity for turning individuals into either predators or parasites. The predators are the rich who live off the labors of the middle and lower classes. The parasites are the poor who live off the table scraps of the middle and upper classes. "Many nations have been enfeebled by wealthy classes that feed . . . off the labors of the poor, while other nations have been weakened by the other extreme of feeding the poor off the labors of the rich," Ben Franklin observed. "Throughout the world, the offspring of many families, both rich and poor, have been taught to despise the rigors of labor by removing from them the need to provide for themselves" (Franklin, 1990, 158).

Both extremes are detrimental to the well-being of any society. The solution is simply to structure society so that everyone who is capable must provide for him- or herself through offering something of value to society. Some might ask, "How do you determine what exactly is of value? Should community members support a writer or singer or poet or artist or athlete? The answer, of course, is: "If they want to." If the community or a business organization chooses to support such individuals, then so be it.

One might argue, though, that in an economy where the majority of people engage themselves in producing only something useful, they could complete all work in half the time we now take, which would enable a writer or singer or poet or artist or athlete to produce something of practical value and still have plenty of time left for creating books or songs or poetry or paintings or sporting events. Most of the "workers" in our economy are not actually producing anything useful. They belong to the immense and inefficient support structure that holds up the sagging weight of capitalism.

Because of this, our present system requires most people to scrape and borrow and fight full time for even the most basic of necessities. "The history of the world," said H. W. Van Loon, "is the record of a man in quest of his daily bread and butter." Why is this so? Because lunch has become just like any other piece of merchandise—instead of being equally available for all, it is hoarded by some and withheld from others.

Our current economy is a predatory system far worse than any seen in nature. Where else but among human predators do individuals try to hoard much more than they can ever use? The human predator, I argue, is unlike all others. Instead of being simply the fulfillment of its own nature, the human predator is to a large degree the product of a system—an artificial environment shaped by beliefs and rules and customs—that allows the predatory tendency to run rampant. If, however, we change the parameters of our environment, we can both rein in these predatory tendencies and unleash many cooperative, benevolent, community-oriented inclinations.

Conclusion

Designing Our Destiny

Long experience teaches us that a developing economy will not simply evolve on its own. Such an arrangement can only be, well, arranged. If we want a developing economy, we must design it. Rather than letting an unlimited growth system simply evolve and consume our lives without any kind of human direction or shaping, we ought to have an active hand in creating an economic system that is consistent with our social and political ideals. The question here is, *Who is in control—the economy or the individuals who participate in it?*

Regaining Control

Robert Pirsig, in *Lila*, describes how his alter-ego, Phædrus, is walking the streets of New York City, fascinated by the manhole covers and marveling at the "staggeringly complex underground networks of systems that made this whole island happen . . . like the nerves and arteries and muscle fibers of a giant organism."

It was spooky how it all worked with an intelligence of its own that was way beyond the intelligence of any person. [Phaedrus] would never know how to fix one of these systems of wire and tubes down below the ground that ran it all. Yet there was some-one who did. And there was a system for finding that person if he was needed, and a system for finding that system that would find him. The cohesive force that held all these systems together: that was the Giant. . . . People look upon the social patterns of the Giant in the same way cows and horses look upon a farmer; differ-ent from themselves, incomprehensible, but benevolent and appealing. Yet the social pattern of the city devours their lives for its own purposes just as surely as farmers devour the flesh of farm animals. A higher organism is feeding upon a lower one and accomplishing more by doing so than the lower organism can accomplish alone. . . . It [is] customary to think of a city like New York as a "work of man," but what man invented it? What group of men invented it? Who sat around and thought up how it should all go together? (Pirsig, 1991, 216)

The answer to Pirsig's question is that no one thought it up, at least not in its present form, and that fact lies near the heart of the trouble. Pirsig sees our collective social patterns as a higher organism than an individual human being—indeed, he sees this as good. A corporation or city or state or country can use up and throw away individuals just as we use up cells and slough them off, and it is a completely moral act, because the social pattern is a higher organism and therefore has higher needs, a higher morality.

It is, of course, this very notion that I am attacking in this book. The social pattern—whether it be a city, a nation, an economy, a government agency, or a business—especially one that evolved unconsciously, is not a higher organism than a man or woman, for the simple reason that it is not a self-aware entity. And the fact that it *evolved* at all, without conscious direction, is merely an indication that we have forsaken the blueprint of the Founders, for the great American experiment that they set in motion was a glorious attempt to *design* and *shape* social patterns so that they serve mankind, rather than allowing them to evolve without direction, in which case they subdue us, and we serve them.

"It has been our complacent boast," asserts David K. Hart, "that since our nation was founded upon a set of specific 'unalienable rights,' our present affairs will obviously reflect the same high standards." Unfortunately, such is not the case. The Giant, the monster, the network of machines, the bastard child—the system—is in control. It has grown up without our attentive instruction, without correct principles to shape its evolution, because we have become an ignorant people—ignorant in matters of moral philosophy and human dignity and equality and liberty and democracy. "To be a principled individual," Hart continues, "has always required both knowledge and moral courage; to be a principled society has always required *sustained* and *intentional* moral effort. But in our headlong rush for prosperity, we have trivialized the ethical standards of our national founding. We have become a 'bedollared nation' at the expense of our national soul" (Hart, 1988a, 3; emphasis mine).

If we are to survive as a nation, and especially if we are to become what the Founders envisioned, we must, in a sense, become Giant slayers or at least Giant tamers. We must regain control of the monster, even if this means executing or at least disabling it. We must exert ourselves in an informed, intentional moral effort and shape our own destiny as a people, instead of allowing our unintentional social patterns to evolve into the worst predator we can imagine.

I call this *the deliberate act of democracy.* For democracy is not a passive political program. Government of the people, by the people, and for the people does not just happen by putting a pattern in place—in our case, the Constitution—and letting social activity unwind like the spring in a clock. Self-government can only happen when a knowledgeable citizenry engages in moral, social, economic, and political discourse, struggles its way to a consensus, and thus shapes its own destiny. We have slipped far from this way of governing, unfortunately, to the extent that an "economy" that has more or less created itself is largely in control of our lives.

Leaders

There is one monumental problem facing us as we strive to shape our social and economic patterns. "We the people" are not simply going to rise up and take back what is rightfully ours. If we tried, we would reap only chaos. Why? Because we have already become a society governed by anarchy more than by democracy. According to Warren Bennis, this anarchy is the direct result of poor leadership. The people in charge have imposed change rather than inspiring it, he says. We've had bosses instead of leaders, and we've finally grown so weary of the charade that everyone has simply decided to be his or her own boss. "Each of us," says Bennis, "is a majority of one" (Bennis, 1989, 63).

We have a lot of people who are disgruntled, even angry, about the current state of affairs, but each in his or her own way. There is nothing that binds us together in our yearning for a better world except our disgust with the status quo. We have neither any kind of consensus, nor any common dream, and we definitely don't have a leader, someone who can pull us all together behind a single vision and lead us to a brighter future.

Where have all the leaders gone? Two hundred years ago, Bennis says, we had a population of 3 million people, yet six world-class leaders contributed to the framing of the Constitution. "Today, there are more than 240 million of us, and we have

Ollie North, the thinking man's Rambo. What happened?" Eighteenth-century America, he contends, was notable for its geniuses, nineteenth-century America for its adventurers and entrepreneurs, and early twentieth-century America for its scientists and inventors. By contrast, "late-twentieth-century America has been notable for its bureaucrats and managers. What those Philadelphia geniuses created and their rowdy successors built, the organization men—in both government and business—have remade, or unmade." These business "leaders" saw our abundance of natural riches, but also saw that they had the mechanical means to develop them, and, "in the rush to do so, they put aside the development of this democracy, along with their own personal development as citizens" (ibid., 33).

This has been the history of America: abandoned dreams. We have always had the potential for true greatness—the blueprint is still there for all of us to read—but we've always been distracted by selfish material concerns. Thus, our uniquely American form of self-interest has now created a virtual anarchy in the land of democracy.

Bennis claims that we've come face to face with our "amazing aspirations" four times in our history, and each time we've come away empty-handed. Most recently—in the 1960s— "everything was in motion again, everything but human nature. We emerged from that tumultuous decade sadder, no wiser, but liberated—free to be me and me, *never* us" (ibid., 45).

It is time, though, to be *us*. Indeed, it is now or never. We must place our individual grievances on the shelf alongside our shopworn self-interest. Democracy demands that we pull together, that we slay the Giant and *deliberately* replace it with the decent, just, free, informed society envisioned by the great leaders whose values and moral certainty we still look to in these troubled times. We are bound to them by ties that even capitalism has been unable to totally sever. Unfortunately, though, we shall not simply pull together like iron filings around a magnet—for we have no magnet. We shall not pull together until dynamic, intelligent, moral leaders step forward and invite us to follow them onto the rugged path of necessity. Only then will we escape total ruin.

> The founding fathers and the adventurers and inventors who succeeded them were dreamers, and dreamers on a grand scale. Today, we do not dream but merely fantasize about money and things. As a dreamless sleep is death, a dreamless society is meaningless. As individuals, we need dreams in the way we need air, and as a society, we need true leaders—uncommon men and women who, having invented themselves, can reinvent America and restore the collective dream by expressing for and to us that irreverent, insouciant, peculiarly American Spirit. (ibid., 39)

I believe those leaders are among us, silent because they have yet to find their voices. Perhaps this book will be of some value to them in this regard. I hope so, and I trust that they will step forward as they find their message, their vision.

Still, the choice we must make is an extremely difficult one—even if a modern-day Washington or Jefferson or Madison or Lincoln were to inspire us in our choosing—and suffering will come regardless of which course we follow. It is truly too late to avert that reality. Still, we must begin to study our predicament with open eyes, so that we can recognize the truth when we hear it, and follow the right voice.

And choose we must. We can pursue our present course and cruise on blindly until we crash into the inevitable iceberg, or we can abandon ship, salvaging what we can to rebuild a society that is fully consistent with the values of our founding. One way or the other, though, American-style capitalism will end—either in Götterdämmerung or in quiet though exhausting reform. For this reason it is imperative that we stop wasting our precious time and energy straightening deck chairs on the *Titanic*. The myriad voices who would waste our time with this distraction are singing a siren song we've all but memorized in the past forty years.

We must finally come to our senses, look beyond capitalism, and determine the kind of society we want for our children and grandchildren. And perhaps in this process of awakening we shall rediscover the American Dream. It is not dead, only buried, neglected, forgotten, fragmented, trampled upon. But dreams are amazingly resilient and difficult to kill. Thank God.

References

Barash, David P. 1992. *The L Word: An Unapologetic, Thoroughly Biased, Long-Overdue Explication and Defense of Liberalism.* New York: Morrow.

Bennis, Warren. 1989. *Why Leaders Can't Lead: The Unconscious Conspiracy Continues.* San Francisco: Jossey-Bass.

Block, Peter. 1993. *Stewardship: Choosing Service over Self-Interest.* San Francisco: Berrett-Koehler.

Chamberlain, Neil W. 1973. *The Limits of Corporate Responsibility.* New York: Basic Books.

Church, George J. 1994a. "Recovery for Whom?" *Time*, April 25.

———. 1994b. "We're #1 and It Hurts." *Time*, October 24.

Daly, Herman E. 1990. "Boundless Bull." *Gannet Center Journal*, Summer.

Daly, Herman E. and John B. Cobb, Jr. [1989] 1994. *For the Common Good: Redirecting the Economy toward Community, the Environment, and a Sustainable Future.* Boston: Beacon Press.

Ferguson, Charles H. 1990. "Computers and the Coming of the U.S. Keiretsu." *Harvard Business Review*, July/August.

Franklin, Benjamin. 1990. *Benjamin Franklin's The Art of Virtue.* Edited by George L. Rogers. Eden Prairie, Minn.: Acorn Publishing.

Frost, Robert. 1969. "The Black Cottage." In *The Poetry of Robert Frost*, ed. E. C. Lathem. New York: Holt, Rinehart & Winston.

Galbraith, John Kenneth. [1967] 1971. *The New Industrial State.* 2d ed. Boston: Houghton Mifflin.

Grossman, Richard L., and Frank T. Adams. 1993. "Citizenship and the Charter of Incorporation." *World Business Academy Perspectives* 7, no. 4.

Hamilton, Alexander, James Madison, and John Jay ["Publius"]. [1787-88] 1982. *The Federalist Papers.* New York: Bantam Books.

Harman, Willis. 1991. "Doing Business in a Transforming Society: Background Notes for Dialogue." Seminar Outline.

———. 1992. "Whatever Happened to Usury?" *World Business Academy Perspectives* 6, no. 2.

———. 1994. Letter to the author. March 3.

Hart, David K. 1988a. "Life, Liberty, and the Pursuit of Happiness: Organizational Ethics and the Founding Values." *Exchange* (Brigham Young University School of Management), Spring.

———. 1988b. "The Sympathetic Organization." In *Papers on the Ethics of Administration*, ed. N. Dale Wright. Provo: Brigham Young University, 1988.

Hawken, Paul. 1993. *The Ecology of Commerce: A Declaration of Sustainability.* New York: HarperCollins.

Heilbroner, Robert L. 1986. *The Worldly Philosophers: The Lives, Times, and Ideas of the Great Economic Thinkers.* 6th ed. New York: Simon & Schuster.

"The Job Drought." 1992. *Fortune*, August 24.

Johnson, Paul. 1992. "An Awakened Conscience." *Forbes*, September 14.

Jonas, Norman. 1987. "Can America Compete?" *Business Week*, April 20.

Jouvenel, Bertrand de. 1962. *On Power.* Trans. J. F. Huntington. Boston: Beacon Press.

Korten, David C. 1991-92. "A Deeper Look at 'Sustainable Development.'" *World Business Academy Perspectives* 6, no. 2.

Adapted by Willis Harman from "Sustainable Development," *World Policy Journal*, Winter 1991-92.

Lasch, Christopher. 1991. *The True and Only Heaven*. New York: Norton.

Leckey, Andrew. 1993. "Only 18% Regard Jobs as Rewarding." *Deseret News*, December 5, sec. M.

Lux, Kenneth. 1990. *Adam Smith's Mistake: How a Moral Philosopher Invented Economics & Ended Morality*. Boston: Shambhala.

Mill, John Stuart. [1848] 1886. *The Principles of Political Economy*, vol. 2, bk. 3, ch. 7. 9th ed. London: Longmans, Green.

Mokhiber, Russell. 1988. *Corporate Crime and Violence: Big Business Power and the Abuse of the Public Trust*. San Francisco: Sierra Club Books.

Nibley, Hugh W. 1983. "Leaders and Managers." In *Speeches*. Provo: Brigham Young University Publications.

———. 1989. "Work We Must, But the Lunch Is Free." In *Approaching Zion*, ed. Don E. Norton. Salt Lake City: Deseret Book Company.

Patterson, James, and Peter Kim. 1994. *The Second American Revolution*. New York: William Morrow.

Pinchot, Gifford and Elizabeth. 1993. *The End of Bureaucracy and the Rise of the Intelligent Organization*. San Francisco: Berrett-Koehler.

Pirsig, Robert M. [1974] 1980. *Zen and the Art of Motorcycle Maintenance: An Inquiry into Values*. New York: Bantam Books.

———. 1991. *Lila: An Inquiry into Morals*. New York: Bantam Books.

Reich, Robert B. 1991. *The Work of Nations: Preparing Ourselves for 21st-Century Capitalism*. New York: Knopf.

———. "High-Wage Jobs Needed to Heal Sick Economy." *Deseret News*, November 5-6, sec. A. Reprinted from *New Perspectives Quarterly*.

———. 1994. "Business Has a Stake in Saving Middle Class."

Deseret News, October 9, sec. V. Distributed by Los Angeles Times Syndicate.

Rosen, Corey. 1991. "The Options Option: A New Approach to Employee Ownership." *Management Review*, December.

Sawyer, Jon. 1994. "Income Gap Becoming an Income Chasm." *Deseret News*. June 5, sec. M. Reprinted from the *St. Louis Post-Dispatch*.

Scott, William G., and David K. Hart. 1989. *Organizational Values in America*. New Brunswick, N.J.: Transaction Publishers.

Shames, Laurence. [1989] 1991. *The Hunger for More: Searching for Values in an Age of Greed*. New York: Vintage Books.

Smith, Adam. [1776] 1937. *An Inquiry into the Nature and Causes of the Wealth of Nations*. Edited by Edwin Cannan. New York: Modern Library.

Smith, J. W. 1993-94. "Wasted Time, Wasted Wealth." *In Context*, Winter.

Steinbeck, John. [1939] 1982. *The Grapes of Wrath*. New York: Penguin Books.

Tichy, Noel M., and Stratford Sherman. 1993. *Control Your Destiny or Someone Else Will: How Jack Welch Is Making General Electric the World's Most Competitive Organization*. New York: Doubleday.

UPI report. 1994. "2.7 Percent Growth Rate Expected in the U.S. Economy Next Year." *Deseret News*, November 30. No author listed.

Ventura, Michael. 1991. "Someone Is Stealing Your Life." *Utne Reader*, July/August. Reprinted from the *L.A. Weekly*.

Welles, Edward O. 1994. "It's Not the Same America." *Inc.*, May.

Will, George F. 1994. "Kerry Exemplifies Double Dilemma of Democrats in 1996." *Deseret News*, December 4, sec. V.

Wood, Gordon S. 1991. *The Radicalism of the American Revolution*. New York: Knopf.

Index